# Child Care

Graeme Snodgrass

Macdonald Guidelines

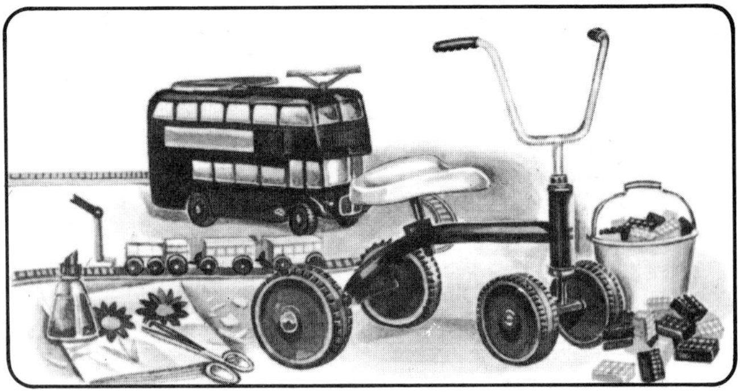

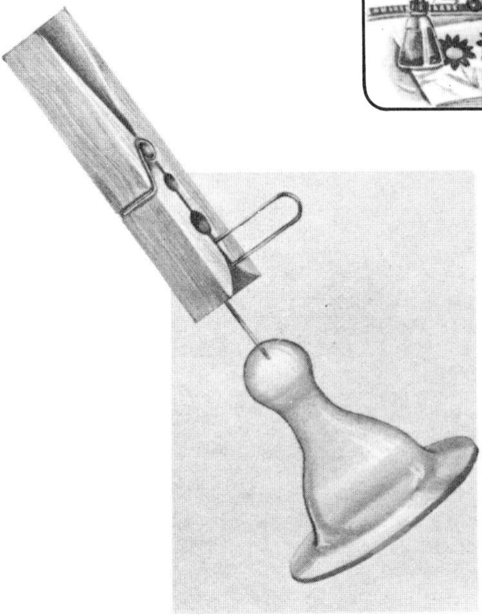

First published 1978
Macdonald Educational Ltd,
Holywell House, Worship Street,
London EC2A 2EN

**ISBN 0 356 06028 4**

Made and printed by
Waterlow (Dunstable) Limited

# Contents

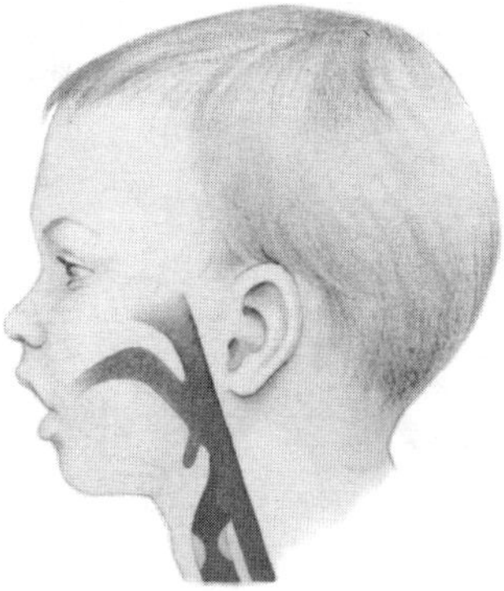

# Early life

The first five years are the most important in life, the period in which the future personality, physical fitness and, in some instances, the very survival of the individual are determined. It would be fair to say that adverse influences have a greater effect in this respect than favourable influences. Each child is born with his own biological potential for growth, intellect and longevity. The potential itself cannot at the present time be improved upon, but environmental influences can modify it so that it cannot be fully achieved. This is especially true during the first two years as far as growth and intelligence are concerned. Such diverse factors as poor nutrition, lack of oxygen when in the womb, serious degrees of jaundice during the first few days of life, infections of the brain and, possibly most important of all, deprivation of normal mothering and loving care may all have a devasting effect upon the child's true potential.

As far as his future personality is concerned, it is the immediate environment of the family that exerts the greatest influence. No individual is born with an inherited capacity for happiness or the ability to get on with, and relate to, other people. These qualities are learned and, not surprisingly, they are learned from those closest to him —the parents. The precise direction towards which the child's personality develops will depend upon the quality of parental care superimposed on certain instinctive drives which he possesses from the time of birth. These drives are common to all humans, may to some extent be inherited and, as with all human characteristics, will vary between individuals in their strength and expression.

Most of the instinctive drives represent evolutionary developments and have been essential factors in survival during the development of the human race. They still have survival value but have a different relevance in modern society. One such drive is that of aggression, which in the relatively effete modern world no longer confers an advantage as it once did in, for example, hunting prowess, but must be channelled into more sophisticated and socially acceptable behaviour. The present-day constraints upon instinctive drives are learned from parents and are re-directed in ways which are unique to the family concerned. Problems and conflicts arise when attempts are made to suppress them entirely.

Nothing can influence the biological potential more than a bad emotional environment; it can affect growth and mental development profoundly, and has a permanent effect on the child's subsequent ability to relate to other people. In short, tenderness, nurture and understanding of the young child is of crucial importance for his future well-being. Fortunately, one does not have to be of high intelligence—or even intelligent at all—to provide these things. A frenzied attempt to do all the *good* things, with all the anxieties and guilt that may thereby result, will count for far less than care to avoid doing the bad things.

This book attempts, within the confines of the space available, to provide some of the basic knowledge and practical information relating to the physical and mental development of the pre-school child, including feeding, health, leisure activities, discipline and safety – the major concerns of every responsible parent.

# The birth

Nowadays, most babies are born in hospital, although for selected pregnancies delivery in the home may be safe and emotionally satisfying for the mother. As hospital confinement is the most usual, some of the typical events are discussed in this section.

After delivery of the head the midwife will usually feel the baby's neck to see if the cord is too tightly wrapped around the neck and, if so, will loosen it. The eyes are quickly cleaned with moistened cotton wool and then the trunk and legs are smoothly delivered. Nowadays the infant is placed on the mother's abdomen so that she can see and touch him while the midwife fixes clamps on to the cord and then cuts it. She will then gently suck the mucus from the back of the baby's throat with a small plastic tube so that he breathes normally right away. If he has not already started crying and breathing deeply this simple manoeuvre will usually do the trick. He is then wrapped in a sterile towel and given to his mother to hold while the afterbirth is delivered. Soon afterwards the baby will receive an injection of Vitamin K, which makes sure that his blood will clot normally. This is routine and does not mean that he is unwell or in any danger.

Very occasionally, the baby may be slow to start breathing; in that case, a paediatrician (children's doctor) may pass a small tube into his windpipe, using an instrument with a light attached, and administer a few puffs of oxygen. Within a minute or two the baby will gasp and then breathe normally. The doctor will then remove the tube, and the baby will be returned to the mother.

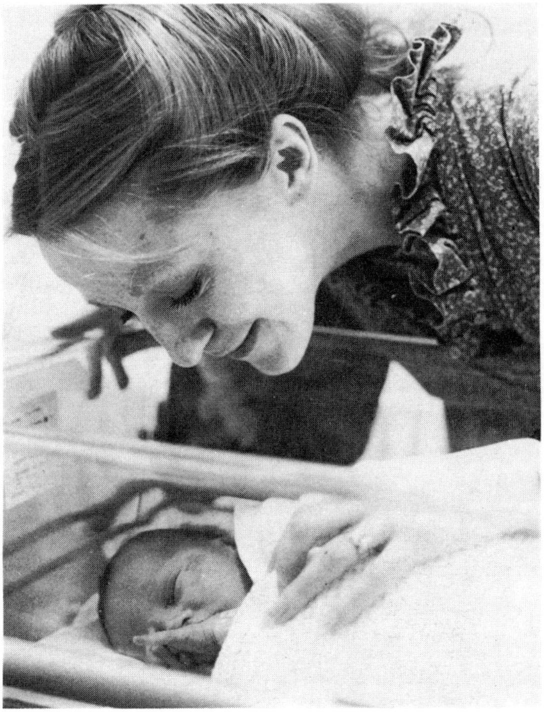

▲ In most hospitals, the mother has her infant close at hand so that she can comfort him if he cries.

Immediately after the birth the baby will not look his prettiest because he will be covered with vernix, a greasy material rather like soft cheese that is cleaned off some time later. There will also be a small swelling over the back of his head with some wrinkling of the scalp. This is called the caput; it is caused by slight compression of the underlying skull bones, which makes the head smaller to allow easier delivery. For this reason the head may be slightly elongated for a few days; soon it will return to a familiar shape and the caput will disappear. The nose and forehead may have a few pearly grey spots which are called milia and are caused by the blockage of small skin glands. They rapidly unblock and disappear. Milia should never be squeezed.

Some babies have little red marks on the skin of the eyelids or between the eyes and at the nape of the neck. These, known as stork marks, are small birth marks that fade and disappear after a few months.

If the mother is dark-skinned, she may find some bluish marks on the baby's buttocks; these look like bruises but they are not. They will disappear without trace during the early months.

Almost all babies pass urine within twenty-four hours of birth. Failure to pass urine after forty-eight hours is very rare and will need investigation. Similarly the first bowel motions should normally occur in the first twenty-four hours. These are dark green in colour, very sticky and called meconium. After milk feeding they change to a yellowish-brown colour.

## Minor problems with new-born infants

Most obstetricians think it important for the baby to be beside his mother as much as possible. This is known as 'rooming in' and serves to increase the mother's contact with her baby – also her confidence. It is better for the baby to be looked after by one person (the mother) than by many different nurses. The mother will then feel more confident in asking questions and

▼ Mothers are expected to be involved in the routine care of their babies when 'rooming in'.

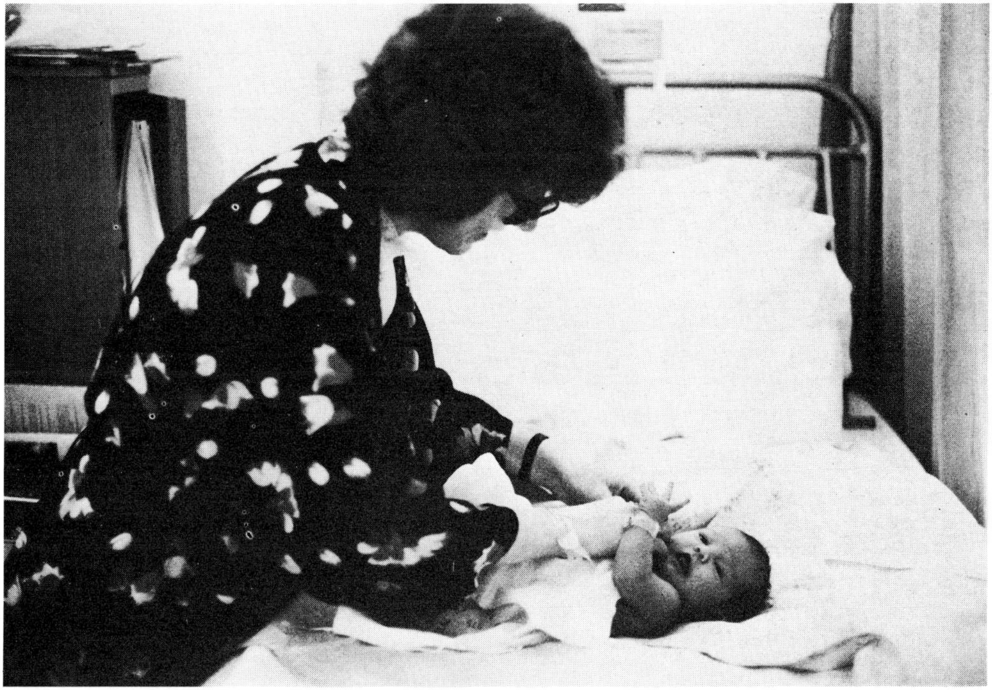

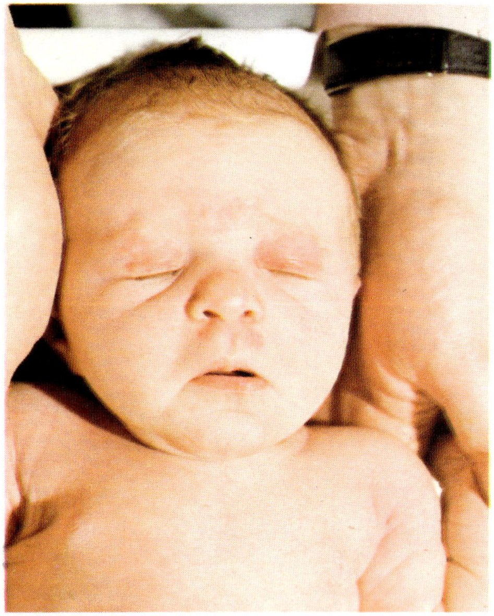

▲ Stork marks are common in the newborn. They are frequently found on the eyelids, in the middle of the forehead and on the nape of the neck. The marks fade within a few months and finally disappear.

generally more at ease. She will, however, notice more about the appearance of her child and see every minor happening, which could cause her to worry. Some common worries are described below.

**Marks on the body** Sometimes, during labour, the mother becomes too tired to push out the baby's head. The obstetrician may then gently apply forceps to lift out the head and also to protect it from being squeezed too hard. Occasionally this procedure leaves red marks on the cheeks, which disappear within a week. A week after such a delivery the mother may feel a tiny lump under the skin of the baby's cheek. This is a small area of congealed fat caused by the pressure of the forceps and will disappear after a few weeks. It is harmless and causes no pain.

**Eyes** The baby's eyes do not open much at first but after three or four days will open more often. A small red mark in the white part may be seen after a difficult birth. This is a small bruise caused by compression of the neck by the cord which causes all veins in the head (and eye) to swell. The bruise rapidly disappears and never harms the eye.

**Breech delivery** If a baby is born bottom-first he may prefer to lie as he was in the womb with his legs straight at the knee rather than bent (as is usual with head-first delivery). After a few days, he will learn to bend his legs.

**Vomiting** This is fairly common during the first twenty-four hours. The vomit, only milk, is caused by the baby swallowing 'liquor' (the fluid surrounding the baby in the womb) during birth. Usually the baby vomits only once, then settles down. If he is sick two or three times, the nurse may pass a tube into his stomach and flush out the liquor. After this there will be no further problem. Green vomiting is not normal and the nurse should be notified of it. It may mean that the baby's intestines are not working properly.

**Jaundice** A yellowish discoloration of the skin occurs in fifteen per cent of all babies. Caused by a delay in the working of the liver, it normally appears on the third day. Only when exceptionally deep in colour is there any cause for concern. Jaundiced infants are usually completely well and will not need further treatment after leaving hospital. The yellow colour usually disappears within fourteen days.

► Babies with jaundice may be a little drowsy and less eager to suck for a few days. Doctors may expose the baby to a blue light in order to diminish the depth of the jaundice.

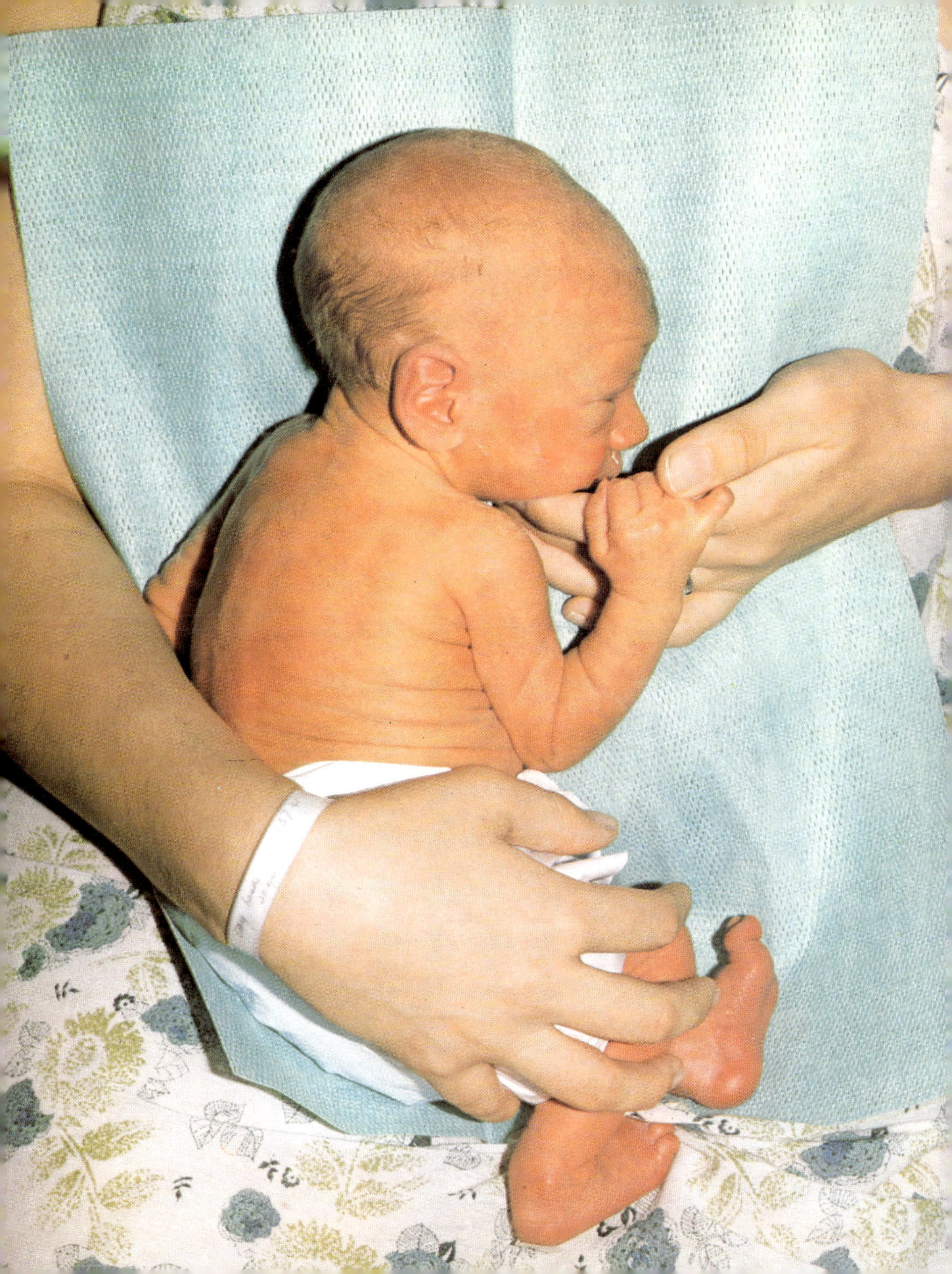

# Very small new-born babies

Infants weighing under 2·5 kg ($5\frac{1}{2}$ lb) at birth are called low-birth-weight infants. They amount to six per cent of all births. Although they are usually premature this is not always the case. A premature infant is one born more than three weeks early. The other type of low-birth-weight baby is described as being 'small for dates'. These babies have usually received insufficient nourishment during the last three months in the womb owing to the placenta not working properly. In consequence they do not grow at the normal rate. The problems of these babies are different from those of the prematurely born.

Both the small-for-dates and the premature may require special care in a nursery staffed by nurses with expertise in looking after very small babies. This may worry the mother, who is likely to imagine the worst and feel helpless. For-

▼ Modern hospital practice is to allow the mother to make contact with her baby even when he requires special care in an incubator. Both mother and child will benefit from such contact.

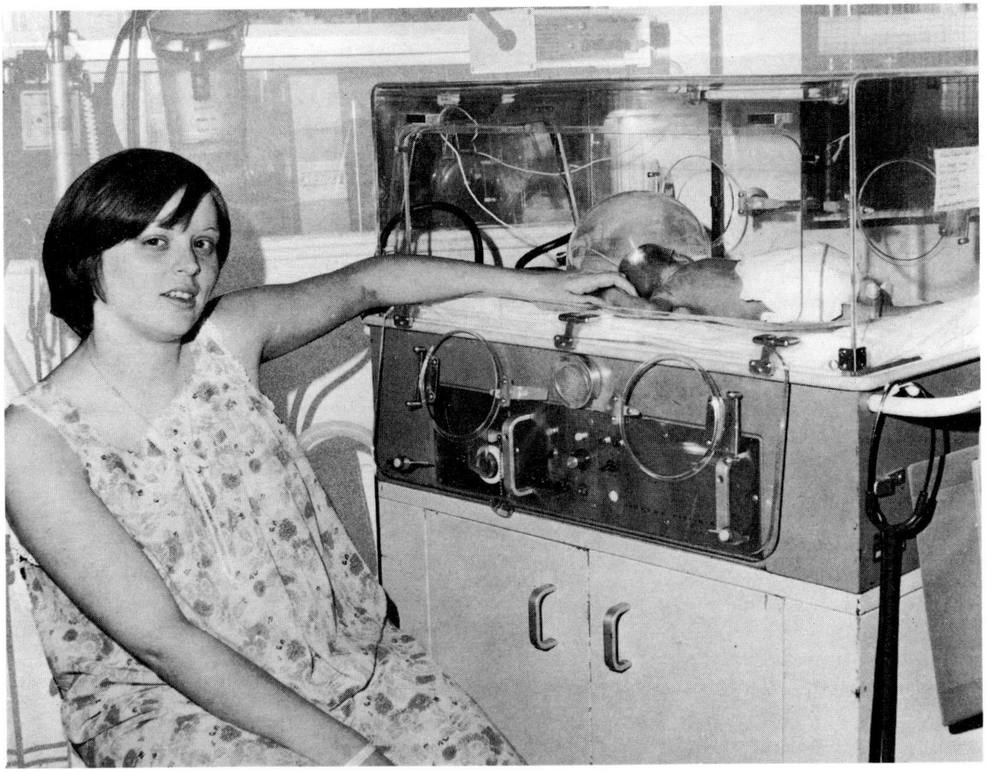

tunately, there is rarely any cause for alarm. The usual reason for the baby's removal is so that a special form of feeding can be started. Nonetheless, some mothers find such separations, so soon after the birth, very worrying. After the baby is settled in the special care nursery, the doctor or the ward sister will return to the mother with a progress report. The next day she will be taken to the nursery to see and touch her infant. As soon as she is ready to walk she can spend much more time in there and will get to know the nurses looking after him.

**Premature babies** These are basically immature new-born infants. They cannot do some of the things which come easily to a full-term baby. In particular, they may not be able to suck, in which case they will be fed by tube. This technique is fairly simple: first, the tube is passed into the baby's stomach by a nurse, then the milk flows from the container to the baby. Many progressive nurseries allow the mother to hold the milk container, to give her a feeling of involvement.

It may happen that a number of blood samples are taken from the premature baby, by pricking his heel. This does not mean he is ill, but is done to ensure he has the right amount of sugar in his blood. If it is too low, extra feeds may be necessary. Occasionally, premature babies develop a breathing difficulty which needs expert treatment, sometimes in a different hospital. This is more common in babies who were delivered more than six weeks early. Sometimes the problem is serious, but the treatment, using special breathing machines, is effective.

**Small-for-dates babies** These are usually more mature than the premature babies and not so likely to develop breathing difficulties. The babies are under weight for their length, although the sucking response will be normally developed for their age. These infants have difficulty in keeping their blood sugar high enough and need extra feeding.

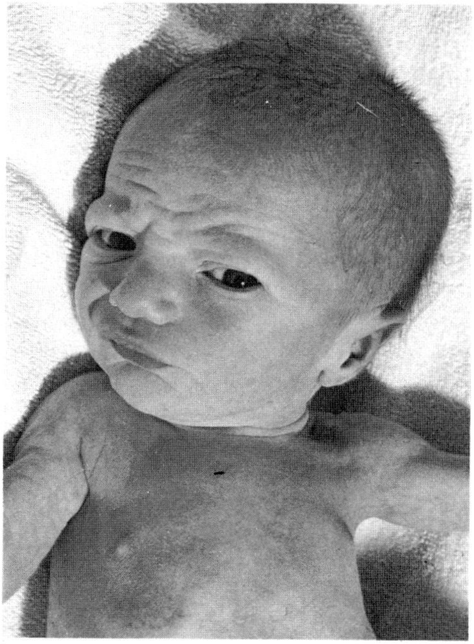

▲ The small-for-dates infant is one who has been under-nourished in the womb as a result of placental failure. At birth, he will look as if he has lost weight and the skin will be loose over his body and face. The loose skin on the face confers a worried-looking expression which is characteristic of these infants.

Both premature and small-for-dates infants are born more commonly to mothers who smoke. Both types may have difficulty in keeping their temperature normal and may become cold. For this reason, they may need to be nursed in an incubator for a few days. Mothers can help prevent low-birth-weight babies by not smoking, by keeping regular ante-natal appointments and by avoiding a hectic life, especially during the last three months of pregnancy.

# Milk feeding

## Breast or bottle?

All children's doctors believe that breast-feeding is the ideal way to nourish the new-born infant. In the past this belief was based on little more than the argument that human milk must be best for humans. Over the past ten years a number of scientific discoveries have provided hard evidence for this belief. In spite of all the good reasons for breast-feeding, only a minority of women do so – and they are largely at the upper end of the social scale. Not all women can breast-feed but almost all who wish to do so will succeed. The key to success lies in the ante-natal preparation. Good obstetric units will prepare the mother for breast-feeding during ante-natal classes. She will be told what to expect after delivery and when that time comes she will be given expert help with the techniques involved.

**Breast-feeding** Mothers who opt for this method will be advised to wear a special nursing brassière. A balanced diet is essential for nursing mothers and should include at least one pint of milk a day. If the mother's nipples are retracted (i.e. not protruding so that the baby can suck easily), they can be made to protract during the last ten weeks by pressing on either side with the thumb and forefinger. A breast shield will also be useful.

After the birth, the infant will be put to the breast frequently during the first two days. During this period the breasts produce a yellowish substance known as colostrum, which is small in amount but of vital importance. It contains a number of antibodies that protect against infection. None of these antibodies is found in artificial feeds. The frequent suckling during this early period stimulates the production of breast milk which 'comes in' on the third day.

It is best to feed the baby on demand rather than to a rigid time schedule. About eight feeds a day are usual over the first week, reducing to six feeds daily if the infant is contented. If there are difficulties or queries, the ward sister should be consulted without hesitation.

Most ward sisters are well versed in the difficulties encountered by nursing mothers. They realize that many women feel rather low after giving birth and that new mothers, in particular, can easily become discouraged by minor problems encountered in breast-feeding. One of these is that of the infant who becomes very drowsy after a few minutes on the breast. This usually happens when a regular time schedule is used for feeding, and indicates that the baby is just not prepared to be fed by the clock. Changing to demand feeding almost always corrects the situation.

Similarly, the hectic activity that is typical of all post-natal wards may unsettle some mothers and affect milk production. In such circumstances, husbands can play an important part by visiting their wives regularly. The presence of someone close to them, who knows exactly how they are feeling, generally has a calming influence.

One slight drawback with breast-feeding is that breast-fed babies are more likely to become jaundiced. Jaundice in infants is rarely a cause for concern, and very seldom requires treatment. Some breast-fed infants will remain jaundiced for rather longer

## Advantages of breast-feeding

**1** The basic biological bond between the mother and the breast-fed child will be stronger because of the greater degree of cuddling and general body-contact. Child battering is commoner where bonding is poor.

**2** Breast milk contains more polyunsaturated fatty acid than cow's milk, which is good for the developing brain.

**3** There is less protein in breast milk than cow's milk. If an excessive amount of a certain protein accumulates in the blood of a pre-term baby, it could, theoretically, cause brain damage.

**4** Certain antibodies are transmitted to the baby in colostrum and breast milk. These antibodies give protection against chest infections and gastro-enteritis.

**5** All babies (and adults) have germs in their large bowel which serve to protect against take-overs by harmful germs. The normal, harmless germs thrive in the slightly acid environment which is provided by breast milk. Cow's milk makes the stools slightly alkaline.

**6** Allergic diseases such as asthma and eczema are caused by sensitivity to foreign (non-human) proteins, such as those found in cow's milk. These diseases are known to be less common in breast-fed humans.

**7** Cow's milk contains four times more salt than breast milk. In certain situations, for example, when a baby is suffering from diarrhoea, feeding with cow's milk may lead to excessive salt levels in the blood. This frequently causes brain damage.

**8** Cot death, where an infant dies inexplicably, almost never occurs in breast-fed babies.

**9** Breast-fed babies are less likely to become obese. Babies who are obese in the first year very often become fat children.

than usual (the normal duration is eight or nine days); occasionally, the condition persists for two to three weeks. There is rarely any cause for anxiety when this happens.

**Bottle-feeding** The single advantage of this method is that it can be done by other people. In practice, this means that the mother can resume her job more quickly, which may be crucial if she has no financial support. Artificial feeds are all derived from cow's milk and today they are modified so that chemically they resemble breast milk. Doctors now prefer the so-called 'filled' milks to the older-established milks, but the choice is fairly limited. The filled milks include SMA, SMA Gold Cap, Cow and Gate Premium, Cow and Gate V formula Plus and Ostermilk Complete formula.

▼ **Weight gain** Normally the infant will lose some weight over the first three days but will then return to his birth weight by eight to ten days. Thereafter he should gain steadily. There is a helpful formula which can be used to calculate this. The age in days minus ten = the number of ounces more than the birth weight, e.g. a 30-day-old baby should have gained 30 − 10 = 20 oz (600 g). The formula is valid up to three months of age. The birth weight will double by age five months and treble by age one year. The graph below shows the gain in weight from birth in ounces according to the infant's age, e.g. by thirty days he will gain twenty ounces.

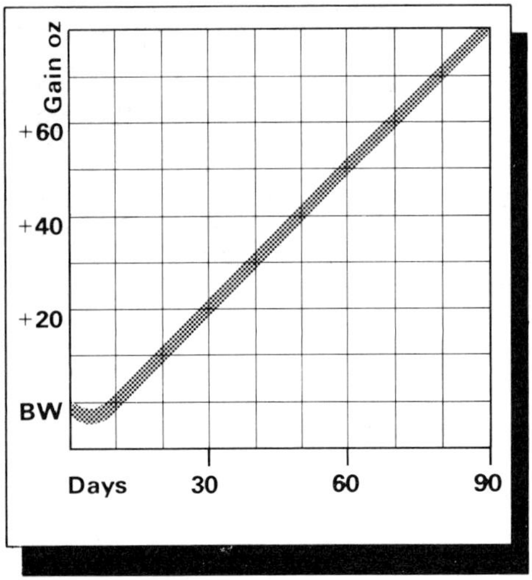


## Preparation of bottle feeds

All mothers who wish to bottle-feed their baby will be shown how to prepare a feed during their hospital stay. As dried milk is cheaper and more convenient to store at home, most mothers opt for it. The instructions on the container should always be read first. The dried milk should be reconstituted with boiled water which has been allowed to become cold. One exact scoop of milk, which has been levelled with a table knife, should be added to 30 ml (1 fl oz) of water. One scoop of dried milk provides 20 calories of energy. Babies need 110 calories per kg body weight per day (50 calories per pound per day), e.g. a 5-kg (11-lb) baby will need 550 calories per day. This can be provided by giving the normal fluid intake of 150 ml/kg ($2\frac{1}{2}$ fl oz/lb) of the reconstituted milk each day from the fifth or sixth day of life.

Feeds should never be made up with heaped scoops of milk powder because this will increase the baby's calorie intake. The excess calories will make the baby fat and will also contain dangerous amounts of salt.

▶ The chart opposite shows the amounts of the various important constituents, such as protein, fat and carbohydrate, for every 100 ml of made-up feed. Note how the constitution of dairy milk exceeds the desirable limits for salt.

**Content comparison of recommended milks**

Human milk has less protein and salt than all other milks but almost the same calorie content. SMA contains slightly more protein and salt than human milk, but Gold Cap contains the same amount of salt. Cow and Gate milks contain much more protein than human milk or SMA milks. Ostermilk Complete Formula contains more carbohydrate than the others and twice as much salt as human milk. Dairy milk has three times more salt and three times as much protein as human milks.

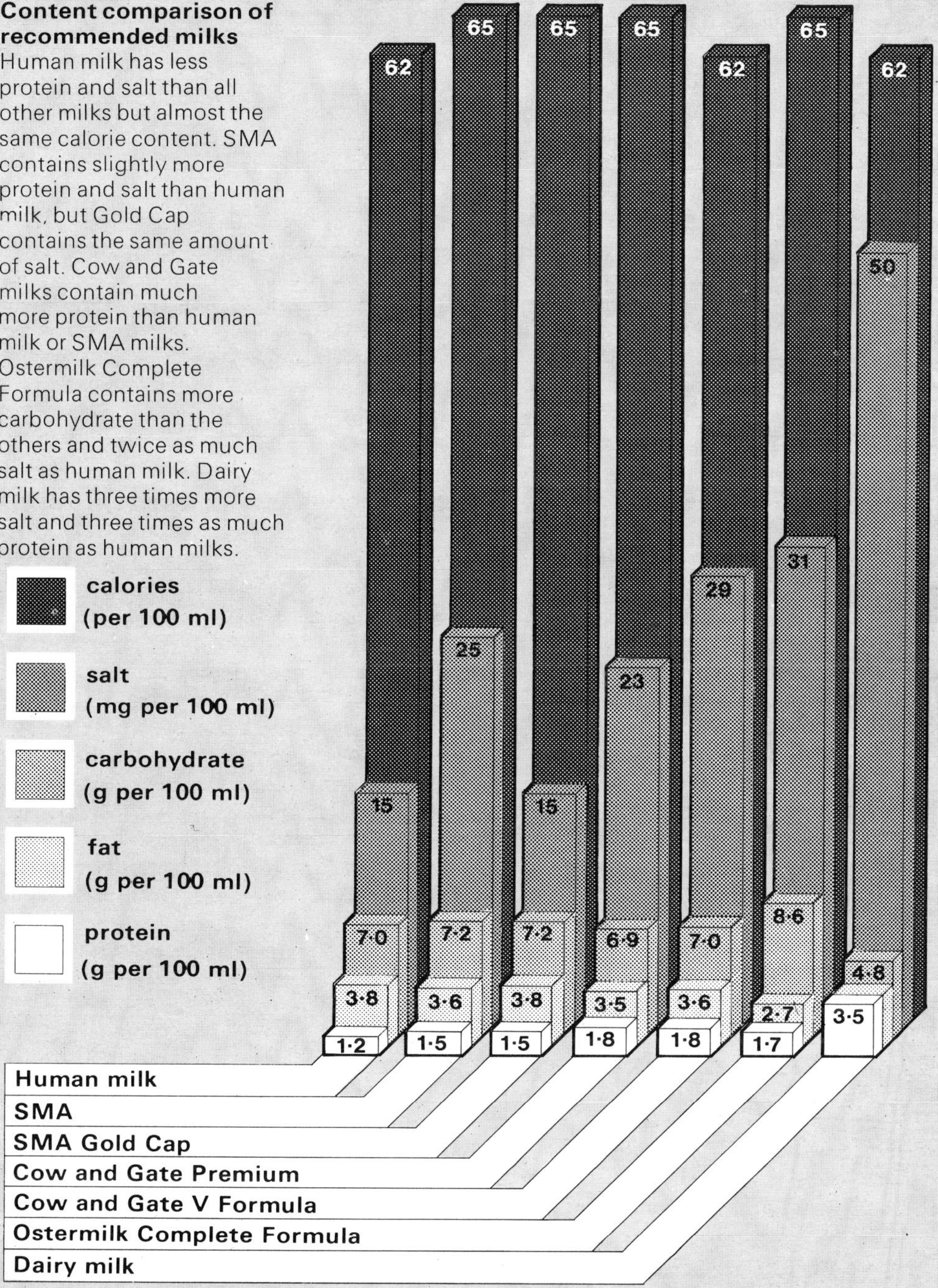

# Screening tests for infants

During the first week of life the baby will be fully examined by a doctor on at least two occasions. These examinations are intended to detect any defects in the baby and help the doctor decide whether any treatment is needed. It is useful to find even minor blemishes which need no attention so that the doctor can discuss them with the mother and answer any question. Any external defects will already be obvious to the mother, who has probably examined her baby as minutely as the doctor!

Internal defects will be carefully checked out by the doctor, by listening to the baby's heart, feeling the abdomen, and so on. Occasionally a heart murmur is discovered. Alarming though it may sound to the mother, a heart murmur rarely means ill health for the baby. Most murmurs at this time are caused by turbulence in the flow of blood through the heart and main blood vessels, rather like noisy plumbing. Most of these murmurs disappear in a week or two, but to be on the safe side the infant will also be seen in the follow-up clinic. Even persistent murmurs generally disappear eventually. Babies who look well but have a murmur seldom have much wrong with the heart. The few that do can easily be treated surgically when much older. Babies with seriously abnormal hearts do not look well and do not thrive.

Babies' hips are always examined carefully because they can occasionally be dislocated. The dislocation is never painful and may not be detected unless specifically sought. If untreated, the hips will never become normal and will require a good deal of surgery and hospitalization. Fortunately the treatment is very simple if detected at birth: it consists of putting three nappies on the baby to keep the thighs apart.

On the sixth day of life a blood sample is taken by pricking the baby's heel. This is for the Guthrie test, a routine procedure for all babies. The test screens for a condition called phenylketonuria which if untreated causes progressive mental retardation. The affected infant does not look ill and if he does not have the test, by the time that the backwardness is recognized it will be too late to put matters right. The damage is caused by an amino-acid (a special type of protein) accumulating in the blood to the point of toxicity. This occurs in the rare infant who cannot dispose of the protein in the normal way. As this amino-acid is present in all milks the process starts soon after the birth. It can be treated with complete success by a special milk, providing it is detected early. The condition occurs in one in 15,000 babies.

In some areas, the first bowel motion (meconium) is examined to test for the presence of cystic fibrosis. This is a condition which produces severe chest infections and causes difficulty in absorbing food from the bowel. Not all doctors are convinced of the value of this test.

Some hospitals test a sample of urine for sugars and protein with a special chemical tablet. The diseases detected by this technique are extremely rare but can lead to mental retardation and failure to thrive properly. Usually the child will show some symptom, such as vomiting, but this is not always the case. Removal from the diet of one of the sugars found in milk can arrest the condition and prevent the complications.

Babies who have had breathing diffi-

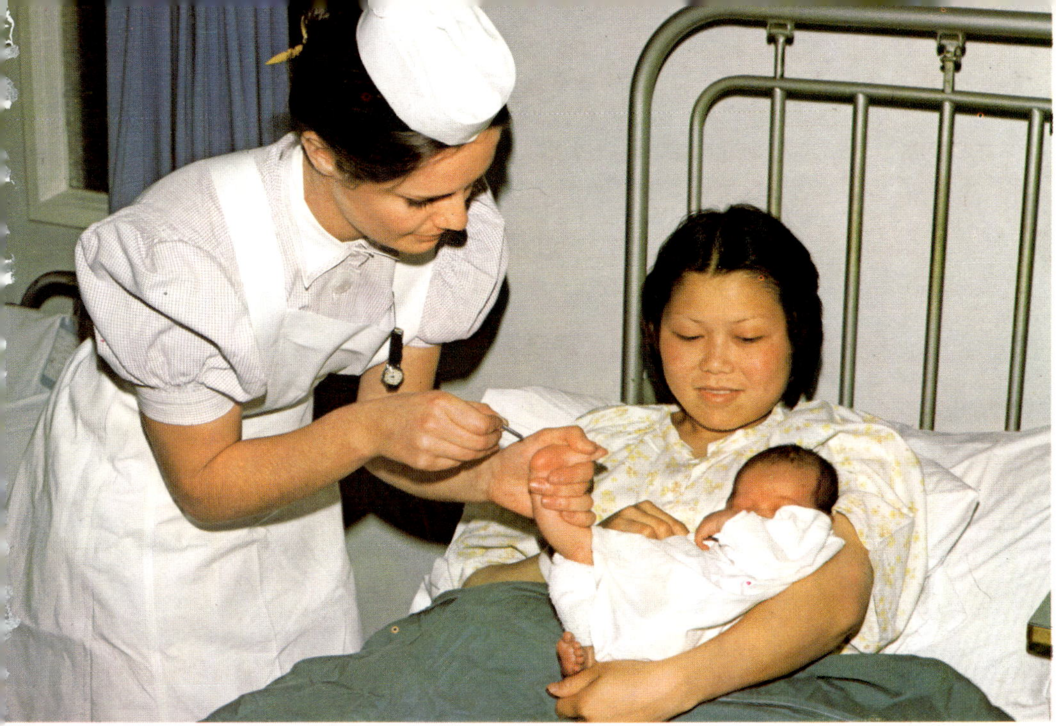

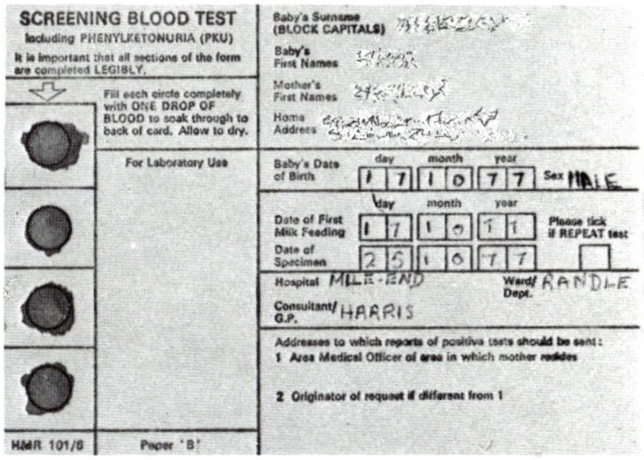

SCREENING BLOOD TEST
Including PHENYLKETONURIA (PKU)
It is important that all sections of the form are completed LEGIBLY.

Fill each circle completely with ONE DROP OF BLOOD to soak through to back of card. Allow to dry.

For Laboratory Use

HMR 101/6 | Paper 'B'

Baby's Surname (BLOCK CAPITALS)
Baby's First Names
Mother's First Names
Home Address

| | day | | month | | year | |
|---|---|---|---|---|---|---|
| Baby's Date of Birth | 1 | 7 | 1 | 0 | 7 | 7 |
| Date of First Milk Feeding | 1 | 7 | 1 | 0 | 7 | 7 |
| Date of Specimen | 2 | 5 | 1 | 0 | 7 | 7 |

Sex MALE
Please tick if REPEAT test

Hospital MILE-END
Ward/Dept. RANDLE
Consultant/G.P. HARRIS

Addresses to which reports of positive tests should be sent:
1 Area Medical Officer of area in which mother resides
2 Originator of request if different from 1

▲ Here a nurse is pricking a baby's heel with a sterilized stilette in order to obtain a few drops of blood for the phenylketonuria screening test.

◀ This is the standard test card upon which the drops of blood are placed.

culties, who were born very much pre-term or who have had oxygen therapy will be examined by an eye specialist before discharge. This is to look for signs of the condition called retrolental fibroplasia, which is caused by excessive amounts of oxygen in the blood. The condition is fortunately very rare nowadays but when severe can cause total blindness.

Finally, the infant is fully examined, for the second time, just before mother and baby leave hospital. This is often done in the mother's presence in order that any minor worries can be discussed and explained. Also, if there is a problem which needs following up in the outpatients' department, the reasons can be explained at the same time.

Usual reasons for a follow-up appointment will include a check on weight gain for those discharged well below the birth weight, checks that minor infections have cleared up or that jaundice which has been deeper than usual has completely disappeared. These safeguards will ensure a good start in life.

# Home with the baby

Most mothers and babies are discharged from hospital after seven to ten days. By then, mothers who are breast-feeding will have received both instruction and supervision from the nursing staff and the infant should be fully established at the breast. Any mother who is bottle-feeding will have been shown how to prepare a feed and told how to sterilize feeding materials (see pages 58-9). She will also have been shown how to bath her child and change his nappies.

**Adjustments at home** The arrival of a new baby very often creates minor anxieties in both the parents and in their other offspring. Knowing that some degree of anxiety is highly likely, the mother should try not to let the situation depress her. However, about ten per cent of mothers do feel depressed after the birth, though they may be unable to describe the reasons for such a feeling. This may show itself as uncharacteristic irritability, bursting into tears, or even undue apathy. Husbands who are aware that this is a common reaction to motherhood may try to be more understanding and helpful, but many do not realize that the new mother needs help. They wait to be asked, assuming she will do so when difficulties arise. If she is more than usually difficult to help or cheer up, the husband should take her to the family

▼ The night feed is often the most relaxed and satisfying of the breast feeds. There are no bottles to fill and father can sleep throughout!

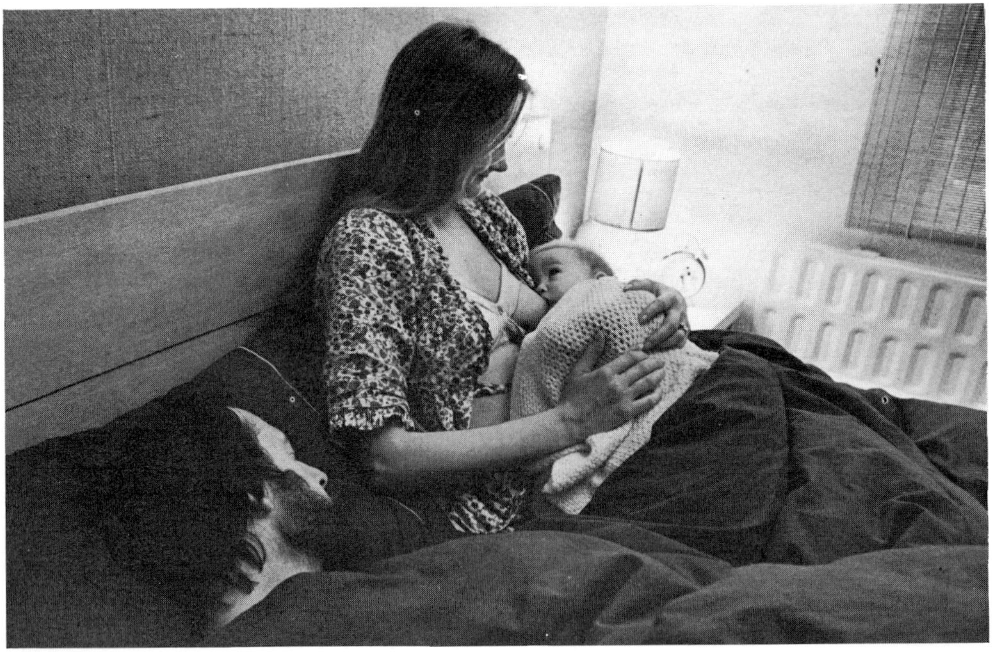

► Winding, perhaps a rather over-rated procedure, can be done in either of the two ways depicted. The most important principle is to keep the baby's back in the erect position in order to allow the air to rise above the fluid level in the stomach. Do not be too vigorous and do not bounce the baby up and down, or you may make him sick.

doctor, for she may be truly depressed and need medical help.

Some fathers, too, may show signs of jealousy. At such a time, a little of the mother's time and attention, away from the baby, can help a good deal. Parents should also try to make arrangements with a suitable person to babysit for at least one evening a week so that they can relax together. It is advisable to make these arrangements before the baby is born as it is not always easy to do so afterwards.

Adjustments to routine are inevitable after the homecoming of the new baby. These will depend on the individual family but if, for example, the baby is fed at 7 am, this will usually leave time for the mother to see her husband off to work or the children to school. On the whole, life is simpler if the child is demand-fed. Soon the pattern of his demands will be obvious; if occasionally awkward, the pattern can be modified! The 2 am feed can cease when the infant fails to wake for it (usually after a month).

On first coming home, a new-born baby will sleep sixteen hours out of the twenty-four, but during his waking hours, it is important to talk to the baby, pick him up frequently and cuddle him. He will cry if he is dirty, hungry or thirsty. Mothers soon learn to recognize the reason for their baby's complaint from his cry.

Brothers and sisters will probably be delighted with the new baby but should only pick him up under careful supervision unless they are old enough to take full responsibility. Some children exhibit minor signs of worry or jealousy, such as occasional bed-wetting, at the arrival of a new brother or sister. These signs of disturbance are usually shortlived, particularly if the mother has taken care to set aside short periods in which she can devote her full attention to the baby's older brothers and sisters to ensure they do not feel left out.

A health visitor will visit the mother and baby at home after ten days. A trained nurse who has undergone further special training, she will help with any problems relating to the baby, answer questions and explain what happens at the infant welfare clinic (see pages 20-21).

# Infant welfare clinics

Infant welfare clinics are provided by the area health authority to supervise the health of pre-school children, especially those up to one year old. There are several such clinics in each health district, geographically distributed so that there is one within easy walking distance of every mother. The clinics are normally the responsibility of the district community physician and the community physician for child health.

Originally, the clinics were set up to advise mothers on feeding and general aspects of infant care before the National Health Service existed. Nowadays they play a much greater role in the area of preventive medicine, supplying the deficiency of 'well-baby' clinics run by general practitioners, who rarely have time to run their own.

The clinics are staffed by health visitors, community nurses and community doctors, all with experience of young babies and their problems. The mother's first visit should be made when her baby is between the age of two and four weeks. The baby will be weighed and any problems with feeding can be discussed. If all is going well, the child will not necessarily be seen by a doctor until he is six weeks old. Before this time, he can be seen by the doctor if need be. A common early problem is that the baby is not gaining weight fast enough. The cause is seldom illness, but usually a minor feeding problem that can easily be sorted out on the spot. Clinic staff will stress the importance of regular vitamins at this time; vitamin drops are available from the clinics. Milk can be purchased at the clinics, too, at the cheapest possible rates, representing a considerable saving on the price of milk from shops. The clinics are not open at weekends, however.

Immunizations against most infectious diseases, such as diphtheria, whooping cough, polio and measles, are given in the clinics. The health visitor will advise when they fall due.

In recent years the clinics have been fulfilling another very important function, which previously received scant attention: screening for handicaps of various kinds. The doctor will examine all infants at the age of six weeks, three months, six months, nine months and twelve months. He will be looking for any deviations from normal progress in what are called 'milestones of development'. Basically this means that any backwardness will be detected early and the infant referred to a specialized assessment centre for expert advice. Motor problems (disorders affecting muscle power or co-ordination) can also be alleviated if found early. At six months the baby's hearing can be tested with reasonable precision. If hearing loss remains undetected the child will be greatly held back in learning to speak and he may even be considered, mistakenly, to be mentally retarded. Hearing defects can often be remedied in special clinics.

The doctor will also be looking out for visual problems. Of these, the most common is squinting, which can cause loss of vision in the affected eye if left untreated.

Clinic doctors are not permitted to treat patients: they act only as diagnosticians. When they detect an abnormality they will refer the child back to his family doctor or to a hospital or special clinic as is appropriate. Many treatable problems are found as a result of the clinic service. The clinics also

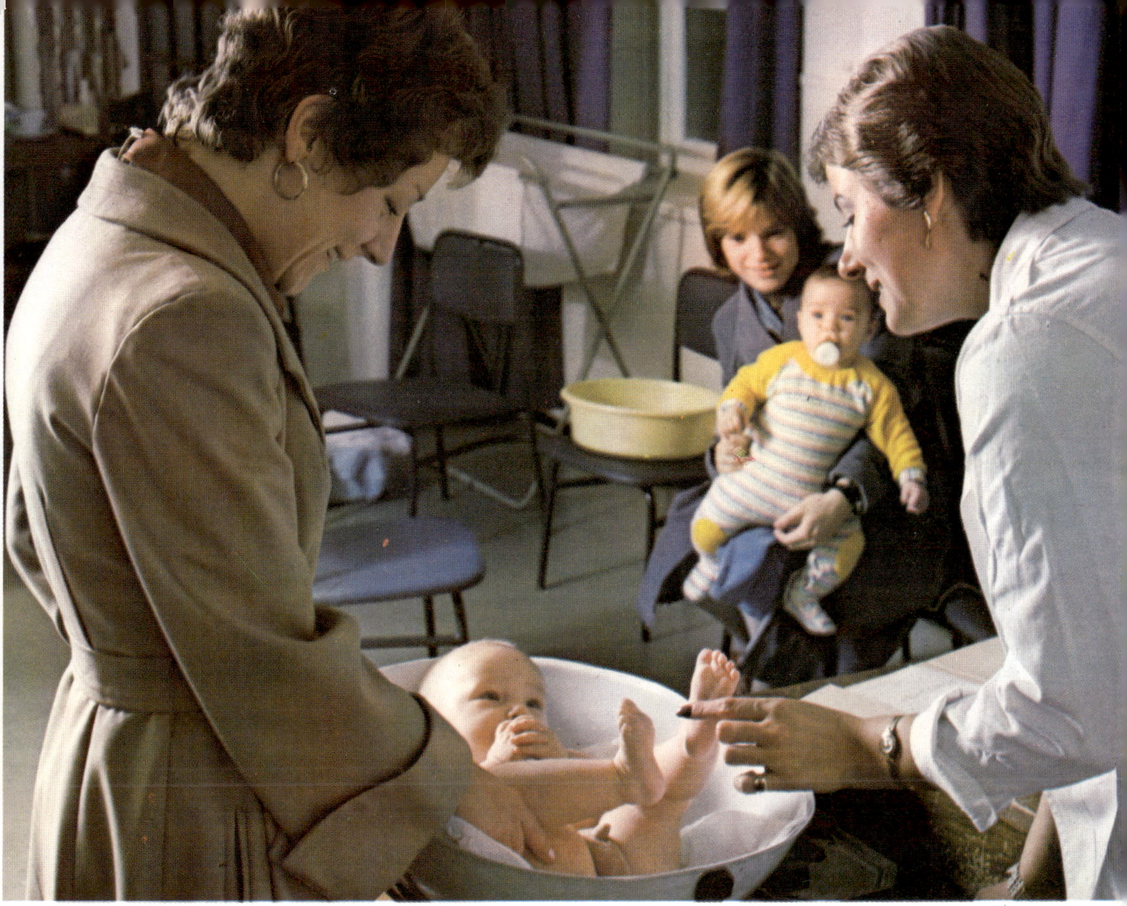

▲ The local infant welfare clinic will first weigh all babies attending before they see the doctor. This provides an opportunity for the mother to discuss minor worries with the health visitor.

provide opportunities for the mother to chat informally to health visitors, nurses, doctors and other parents.

Attending the infant welfare clinic is always worth while. Indeed, in many countries the financial savings to be made on milk and other necessities are substantial. In this respect and many others, the clinics play a strong part in promoting child health in the community.

## Immunizations

The purpose of immunization is to make infants immune and therefore unsusceptible to certain potentially fatal or disabling diseases. It is an artificial way of making the child produce antibodies against a particular germ or to the poisons elaborated by it. This is done by introducing to the baby's system either a killed germ or a live germ. The baby's body will recognize the killed germ as a live one and react by producing antibodies (whooping cough immunization is an example of this). The live germ can either be of the same family as the germ which produces the disease, but completely harmless, or it can be the germ of the actual disease against which the child is to be immunized. In the case of the related germ, because the body cannot always distinguish between similar types of the same germ it will produce an antibody which deals with all of them (examples of this type of immunization include smallpox and polio). In the case of the real germ, it is first substantially weakened by a series of chemical treatments which make it unable to produce the disease but able to stimulate the antibodies. Measles immunization is produced in this way.

Immunization provides complete protection against diphtheria and polio, while the diseases themselves kill or permanently cripple. These immunizations are completely safe. Laziness and irresponsibility on the part of the parents are the only reasons why not all children are immunized. Even measles, it should be remembered, can still kill. If all children were immunized against these diseases, they would cease to exist.

Whooping cough immunization is a less straightforward matter, because it may cause brain damage in one child out of 300,000-500,000. The disease is a major killer of babies in some under-developed countries where immunization is not given, whereas in Britain in 1976 only three children died of whooping cough. Without mass immunization, the figure would have been far higher. Current opinion indicates that whooping cough immunization should not be given to any child who has had a difficult birth or fits. The ultimate decision however rests with the parents.

A schedule for the timing of immunizations is given on page 81.

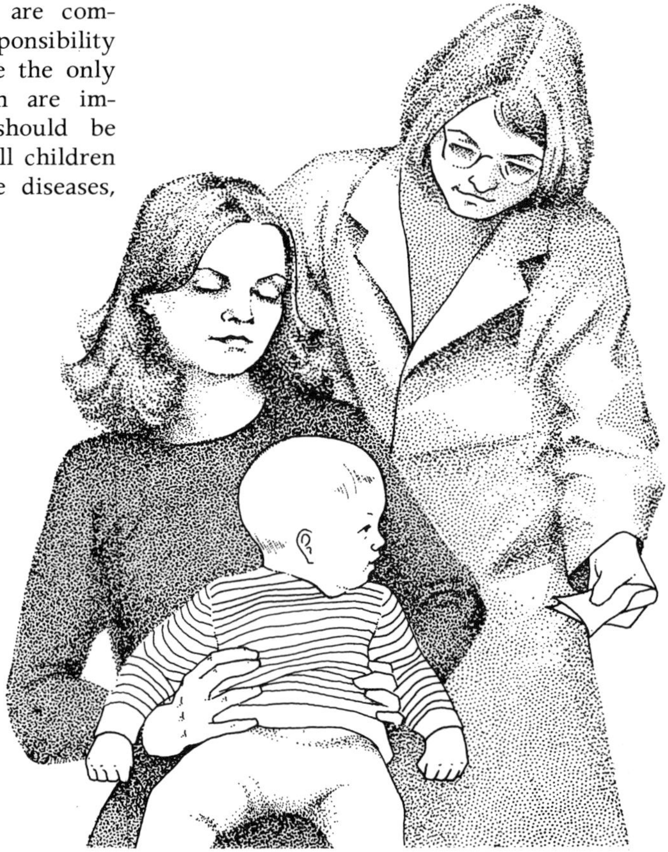

▶ The hearing is routinely tested in the infant welfare clinic when the baby has reached six months of age. The test is designed to assess his ability to hear high-pitched sounds such as the rustling of glossy tissue. By this age, he should turn his head to the source of this sound.

# Development to six months

It frequently comes as a surprise to new mothers that so many new skills are acquired by her baby over the first six months of life. She should beware of statements such as, 'They don't do much until they are sitting up'. These comments usually originate from women who have no experience of babies, or worse, are unobservant and unimaginative. The general achievements during the first year of life cannot and should not be hurried. However, absence of normal stimulation results in delayed progress.

Stimulation includes talking to the baby, holding and 'loving' him and allowing him to look around at what is going on. Denial of these experiences may happen if the mother is depressed after the birth, is simply unaware of the baby's needs, or has placed the baby with an unsuitable childminder while she goes out to work. Babies sometimes lack stimulation when they are hospitalized for a period following the birth. It is, after all, much better for the baby to have his needs met by one or two familiar people than by a large number of different people on the hospital staff.

Here is a general guide to what can be expected from a baby during his first six months.

**Age one week** The baby will look towards a source of light and will briefly follow the movement of a face with his eyes, providing this is less than a metre away. If the cheek is stroked with a finger (or nipple), he will turn his head towards it and open his mouth. This is the 'rooting' response which serves to locate the food source. In response to a sudden noise he may arch his back and extend his arms, opening out his fingers, then bringing his arms across his chest. This is known as the Moro, or 'startle', response. All normal babies do this.

Another interesting development is the stepping reflex, sometimes known as primary walking. This can be produced by holding the baby erect and allowing him to place his feet on a flat surface such as a table top. He will then make stepping movements, which can be accentuated by lifting up his chin a little. This in fact has nothing to do with true walking. Like the startle response, it will normally disappear by three months.

Obviously the baby's muscle power in the early months will be much less than in the older child; at first, he will not be able to hold his head up, except for a second or two when held horizontally by a hand under the abdomen.

Nowadays, most hospitals prefer babies to be nursed prone, so that they can breathe more easily and also so that there is less chance of the baby inhaling milk should he vomit. Because of this, babies usually prefer to lie on their abdomens, with their knees drawn up under them and their heads turned to one side. The feet are usually splayed out in this position.

**Age six weeks** By now, there will have been a number of new achievements, the most important of which, to the mother, is the onset of smiling. This may be noticed at as early as four weeks and does not seem to be related to anything in particular. Frequently, the smile is followed by a burp. This leads many mothers to call it 'smiling with the wind'. In fact, it is the beginning of true smiling and after no more than two weeks is followed by definite smiling in response to the mother's face. This is the first real social response, combining the ability to see mother, recognize her, experience pleasure in seeing her and, most important of all, to express that feeling of pleasure. Because the prerequisites for smiling are complicated, it is not surprising that this is a very important milestone in development. (Marked delay in smiling may be found in babies who were very premature, those who have been very ill during the first month, the mentally backward and the blind.) Normally, at six weeks or so, a baby will also quieten and become still for a few moments when his mother coos or makes soothing noises to him. He will also look at his mother intently when being fed or cuddled.

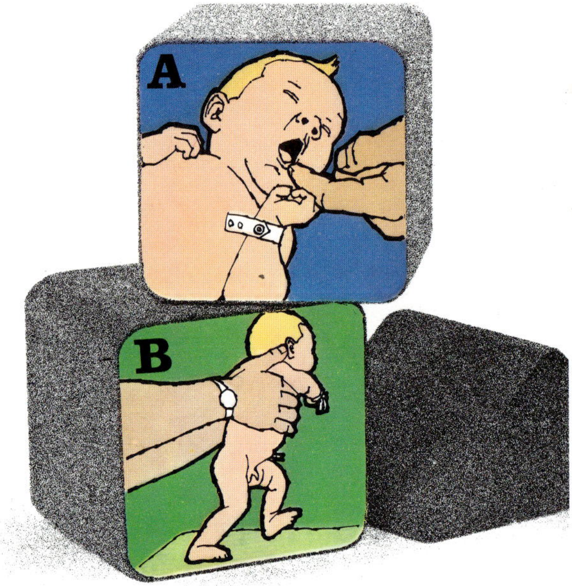


**Age nine weeks** The baby will now make short cooing noises when smiling and show interest in his immediate surroundings up to a distance of about two metres. He will also be able to lift up his head when lying prone, rather than just turning it to one side.

**Age three months** By now, he will be very responsive. He will babble when at rest and may turn his head towards familiar sounds. Many infants will turn towards certain sounds at this age, but apparent failure to do so does not imply deafness. Visual experiences are more interesting than sounds, so, given a choice, he will ignore a sound and concentrate on sights of interest to him provided they are not too far away. By now, the baby may support himself on his forearms, with his head and chest partially raised, when on his abdomen. In this position, he will be more able to see things around him. His control of head movements will also be much more sure, and when held in the sitting position he will be able to hold his head up rather than letting it flop about uncontrollably.

**Age four months** Head control will be good, but if the body is moved suddenly, the head will wobble. The baby will sit happily when adequately propped and will enjoy being in a baby chair. He will now laugh with pleasure and display great interest in people and things around him. He will study his outstretched hands, especially when holding them up in front of a light source. He will clutch at small objects placed in his hands and shake them.

**Age five months** The head will no longer wobble in the sitting position when the baby's body is moved. The baby will readily accept proffered objects in either hand and bring them towards his mouth. When he sees his image in a mirror he will smile and chuckle. He will be very vocal

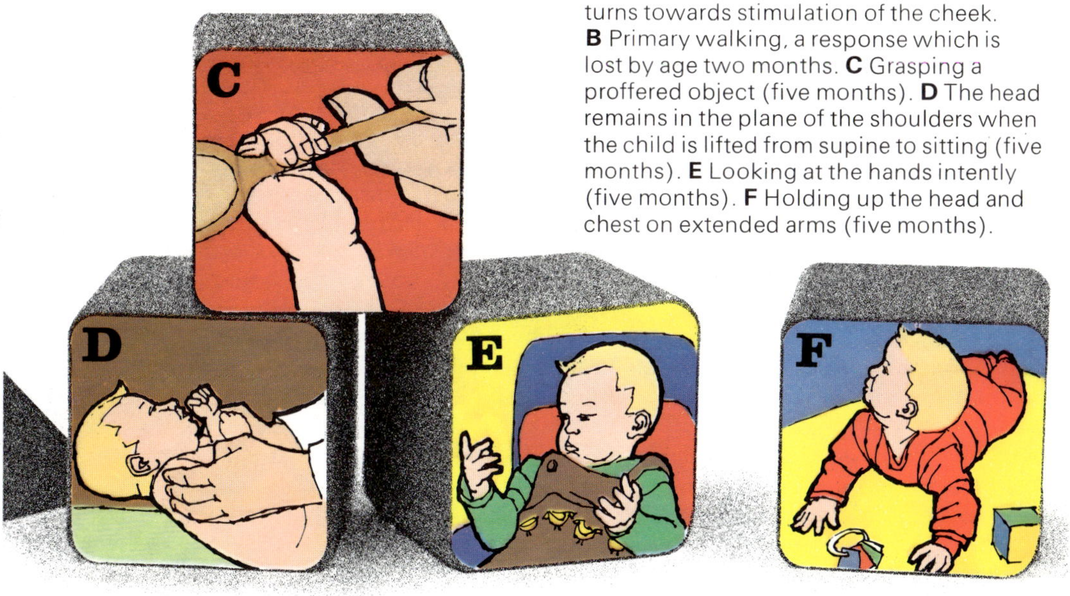


**A** The rooting response, where the baby turns towards stimulation of the cheek. **B** Primary walking, a response which is lost by age two months. **C** Grasping a proffered object (five months). **D** The head remains in the plane of the shoulders when the child is lifted from supine to sitting (five months). **E** Looking at the hands intently (five months). **F** Holding up the head and chest on extended arms (five months).

and babble incessantly, experimenting with various sounds.

**Age six months** By now, the baby will reach out his arms in anticipation of being picked up. He will prop himself up on fully outstretched arms when on his abdomen and will also be able to roll over on to his back. The feeding bottle will often be grasped with both hands and annoyance will be expressed if it is removed too soon. If the baby is held in the erect position he will place his feet on a flat surface and support almost all of his weight. He will lose interest in his hands more quickly and become preoccupied with his toes. Reaching out and grasping objects will please him. He will not yet sit without support.

## Physical changes

By the age of six months some infants will be close to cutting their first teeth. The timing of this process varies a great deal. The usual pattern is for the lower front teeth to become obvious under the surface of the gums, which may become red just before the teeth break through. This is sometimes mildly painful but causes no other symptoms.

The hair at birth, which is of a different quality from that at six months, gradually disappears over the first two months. The hair may seem rather sparse for a while until, at six months, the permanent hair appears.

The head is still relatively large for the body at six months, because the brain is growing rapidly and the skull enlarges to accommodate this growth. The 'soft spot' (anterior fontanelle) is still present but may be only the size of a finger-tip. The body will usually be at its plumpest at six months. However, huge rolls of fat are abnormal at this age and in fact at any other stage of childhood.

# Ailments from birth to six months

The common infectious diseases such as measles, chickenpox, mumps and German measles (rubella) are rare during the first six months. This is because the mother has usually had at least three of these diseases and her antibodies have been passed through the placenta to her unborn child. These antibodies provide protection for the first few months but then disappear, rendering the child susceptible thereafter. The infant of under six months will however be susceptible to other viruses and bacteria with which the mother has not been infected or of which the antibodies were too big to cross the placenta. In practice, these most commonly cause nose and throat symptoms, chest symptoms or diarrhoea.

**Upper respiratory infections** Infections of the upper respiratory tract are those affecting the nose, throat, ears and larynx. The symptoms include nasal discharge, sneezing, a cough with irritability and a reluctance to take all of the feeds. The infections, usually caused by viruses which do not respond to antibiotics, are mild in nature and clear up within a few days. The lungs are rarely affected. If this is her child's first illness, the mother will probably be worried and want to see her family doctor. Once she has seen the infection through, she will be happier about coping with similar infections.

**Lower respiratory infections** These affect mainly the bronchial tubes (bronchitis) or the lungs (pneumonia). Bronchitis does not damage the lungs. Pneumonia is serious but with modern treatment, and if not left too late, rarely kills. A rapid breathing rate will be noticeable. An infant with pneumonia will usually be admitted to hospital unless the family doctor is willing and able to visit him at home frequently.

Another lower respiratory infection which causes rapid breathing is bronchiolitis. This is an infection of the smaller bronchial tubes in which the infant will be seen making violent attempts to breathe. Such infants should always be treated in hospital. With proper treatment, bronchiolitis is rarely fatal. Affected babies are usually breathing normally within three days and out of hospital in a week.

**Gastro-enteritis** This is an infection of the small bowel of which the prominent symptom is diarrhoea. The bowel motions of an affected child are characteristically watery and usually occur more than six times a day. As the bowel motions of all young infants are loose by comparison with those of adults, it is important to realize that it is the high fluid content of diarrhoea which is abnormal. Such fluid loss from the bowel, if allowed to continue, may make the baby dehydrated. As milk aggravates the fluid loss from the bowel, it is essential to stop feeding it to the affected infant. Instead, he should be given boiled water to which sugar has been added. The correct amount of sugar to add is 4 g (1 teaspoon) to 90 ml (3 fl oz) of the boiled water. This should be given for the next twenty-four hours, by which time the diarrhoea should have stopped. The baby can then be given half-strength milk for a further day, after which he will usually be able to take normal feeds of milk again. If the diarrhoea continues as severely as before, in spite of the infant's having been fed boiled water, or if he is vomiting repeatedly, medical advice should be sought. Another danger

**When to call the family doctor**

**1.** If the child vomits all food *and* fluids.
**2.** If there is persistent *watery* diarrhoea even when the child has taken only sugar water in the previous 24 hours; if the diarrhoea is accompanied by vomiting of fluids; if a child suffering from diarrhoea begins to breathe very rapidly.
**3.** If there is coughing, fever and rapid breathing (more than 40 breaths per minute). If the child's tongue and lips are blue (emergency).
**4.** If he complains of headache and is troubled by light. If an older child cannot put his chin on his knees or a younger child (less than two years) is in obvious pain when he moves his neck.
**5.** If he is continually drinking (perhaps waking at night to do so) and passes urine very frequently. If in addition to these symptoms he is breathing rapidly and deeply (emergency).
**6.** If there is a sudden attack of intense lower abdominal pain in his right side accompanied by vomiting. If abdominal pain lasts more than one day.
**7.** If the child has a fit lasting more than five minutes without complete recovery of consciousness.
**8.** If there is a pronounced crowing noise when the child breathes in. If he is having to work hard to breathe, with a heaving chest (emergency).

sign is rapid breathing, which will mean that the baby has too much acid in his blood (acidosis). Most acid is removed from the body by the passage of urine, of which the dehydrated patient will pass very little. Usually, diarrhoea is a mild condition, rarely needing hospital treatment.

**Urinary infection** Not a common problem, this is characterized by poor feeding, vomiting and mildly increased temperature. There are no other symptoms. The condition cannot be diagnosed unless a sample of urine is taken and sent to a laboratory where it can be cultured and the germ responsible identified. This process takes at least two days. Treatment is simple and effective.

Apart from infections, certain more minor afflictions may occur.

**Napkin rash** This will show as a sore, red area around the buttocks and groin. It may sometimes be caused by thrush or by prolonged soaking in urine or stools. In the latter instance, germs on the skin break down one of the constituents of urine (urea) and release ammonia, which has a characteristic smell. Prevention depends on frequent nappy-changing and drying of the area. Polythene pants, which tend to keep the urine in contact with the skin, should not be used too often. General practitioners can easily treat napkin rash. Use of a barrier cream will prevent its return.

**Constipation** Difficulty in passing bowel motions is not common but as long as it is not causing obvious pain there is nothing to worry about. It should not be treated with laxatives. Occasionally a small split in the lining of the anus (an anal fissure) may cause acute pain on moving the bowels and loss of minute amounts of blood. Usually the split will heal if medicine to soften the stool is given. Occasionally, the anus may need stretching by a doctor.

**Blood in the stools** This is usually a trivial matter, caused by a tiny vein breaking just inside the anus. No treatment is necessary. If blood is seen in every bowel motion (very rarely the case), the problem should be given medical attention.

**Black motions** If these are tarry they indicate bleeding high up in the bowel, and the blood is no longer red by the time it is passed. The problem needs medical investigation. However, note that iron medicine will also cause blackening of the motions, which in this case is harmless.

# Development from six months to one year

As the range of developmental attainments varies between infants, precise month-by-month details are inappropriate. There is no such being as an 'average infant', as far as skills go; most babies tend to be advanced in some areas, slower in others. However, within each three-month period certain milestones are generally reached. For example, infants generally manage to sit unsupported at any time from six to eight months. A doctor would be concerned if this had not been achieved by nine months, unless of course the infant had been premature.

**Age nine months** By now, the infant will be able to make chewing movements and cope with a biscuit very well. He will be able to transfer objects from hand to hand without difficulty and will take any new thing to his mouth. He will enjoy reaching out for new objects and exploring them with hands and mouth, and will frequently throw them to the ground. If an object is thrown to the ground he may look for it. This behaviour is especially noticeable if the baby is in his pram. If the object (perhaps a soft toy) is returned to him, he will throw it out again and again. If a toy is taken from him and hidden under a cushion while he is still watching, he will not be able to locate it unless he is very advanced. At this stage hidden objects do not exist and 'out of sight' means out of mind as far as inanimate objects are concerned.

The child will be able to sit without support by this age for periods of up to

fifteen minutes. At seven months he will often use his hands to steady and support himself, but by nine months he will be able to sit and manipulate a toy from hand to hand. Delay in sitting up may be due to premature birth, prolonged illness or weakness of the spinal muscles. A straight back is essential for good sitting posture and this in turn requires good spinal muscles. Weakness of the back muscles results in a hunched posture with the arms used continually for support. This is of course the posture adopted when the infant is just beginning to sit on his own, at about six months, and is therefore unusual at nine months.

Some infants who are late in sitting unsupported may have cerebral palsy (spasticity); others may have received inadequate stimulation from the mother, and may have been left for hours at a time in their cot or pram. Under-stimulated children frequently show evidence of this by having a bald patch on the back of the head.

By now, the child will now be able to localize sounds not only to left and right (achieved normally within six months), but also sounds arising above his head. He will use his voice as a means of deliberately summoning attention, and will express pleasure at the instant response of the mother. Recognition of other members of his immediate family will be well developed and he will behave differently in their presence.

He will not be able to stand properly yet but will be able to stand holding on to the sides of his cot when placed in that position. He will also be able to lift up his head a little when lying on his back. He may also show signs of beginning to crawl at this age, though this tends to occur between ten and twelve months.

**Age twelve months** Crawling will now be both skilled and rapid. Normally, babies crawl on all fours, but variations are fairly common. Some children lie on their faces and make swimming movements. Some infants do not crawl at all but shuffle around on their bottoms. Children who do this usually stand up and walk later than normal. Furthermore, the later they begin to shuffle, the later they will walk. There is rarely any medical reason for this; however, it often runs in families. Such children sit unsupported at the normal time and for unknown reasons will dislike being placed in the prone position (face down). Attempts to place them in the standing position will also be resented and they will draw up their legs and express disapproval. Sometimes these otherwise perfectly normal children will not walk unaided until two years.

Although a normal child is usually sitting on his own by eight months, he will not, at that time, be able to elevate himself

**A** Taking objects straight to the mouth (six months).
**B** Sitting without support (six to eight months).
**C** Looking down from the high chair for a discarded toy. **D** Pulling himself into a standing position (ten to twelve months).
**E** Responding to his mother's voice by mimicry.
**F** Crawling (beginning at ten to twelve months).

▲ At twelve months, the child may be aware that the sweet has been covered by the cup, but he will raise the cup and look inside it, failing to observe that the sweet is still on the table.

to the sitting position. He will normally have achieved this at one year, by which time he will also be able to pull himself up to the standing position, using the bars of his cot or play-pen. When he is tired of this activity he will let himself down with a bump on to his bottom. He will find throwing objects increasingly pleasurable and, in view of the fact that by now he will be able to drink from a cup and feed himself with his fingers, this will prove rather messy! The child's ability to use his hands will be quite well developed by now, and his finger movements will be more precise. He will be able to use his forefinger and thumb (pincer grasp) to pick up small objects accurately.

The child's visual alertness will be highly developed and his curiosity will be provoked by any new sight. He will pay detailed attention to any activity within about four metres. It will be difficult, however, to interest him in activities beyond five metres away: he will divert his gaze to something nearer. Any object within reach will be of great fascination and parents must take care to keep dangerous objects (for example, a hot cup of tea) well out of his reach. By now, the infant will have a much better appreciation

of the fact that objects which are concealed in front of him are not 'gone' and can be found. The process will not be complete, however: if a sweet is hidden under an upturned cup he will lift the cup and look inside it.

He will recognize his name and turn his head when called. His speech will be more organized by this time and he will say two to three recognizable words with meaning, usually 'Mum', 'Dad', 'Nan' and 'no'. He will understand simple commands such as 'Say bye-bye', and will demonstrate by waving his hand.

He will be very responsive to affectionate gestures and, most rewarding of all, will be able to show affection in return.

▼ The first steps taken without support are naturally shaky: mother or father should be near at hand to protect the child from possible falls.

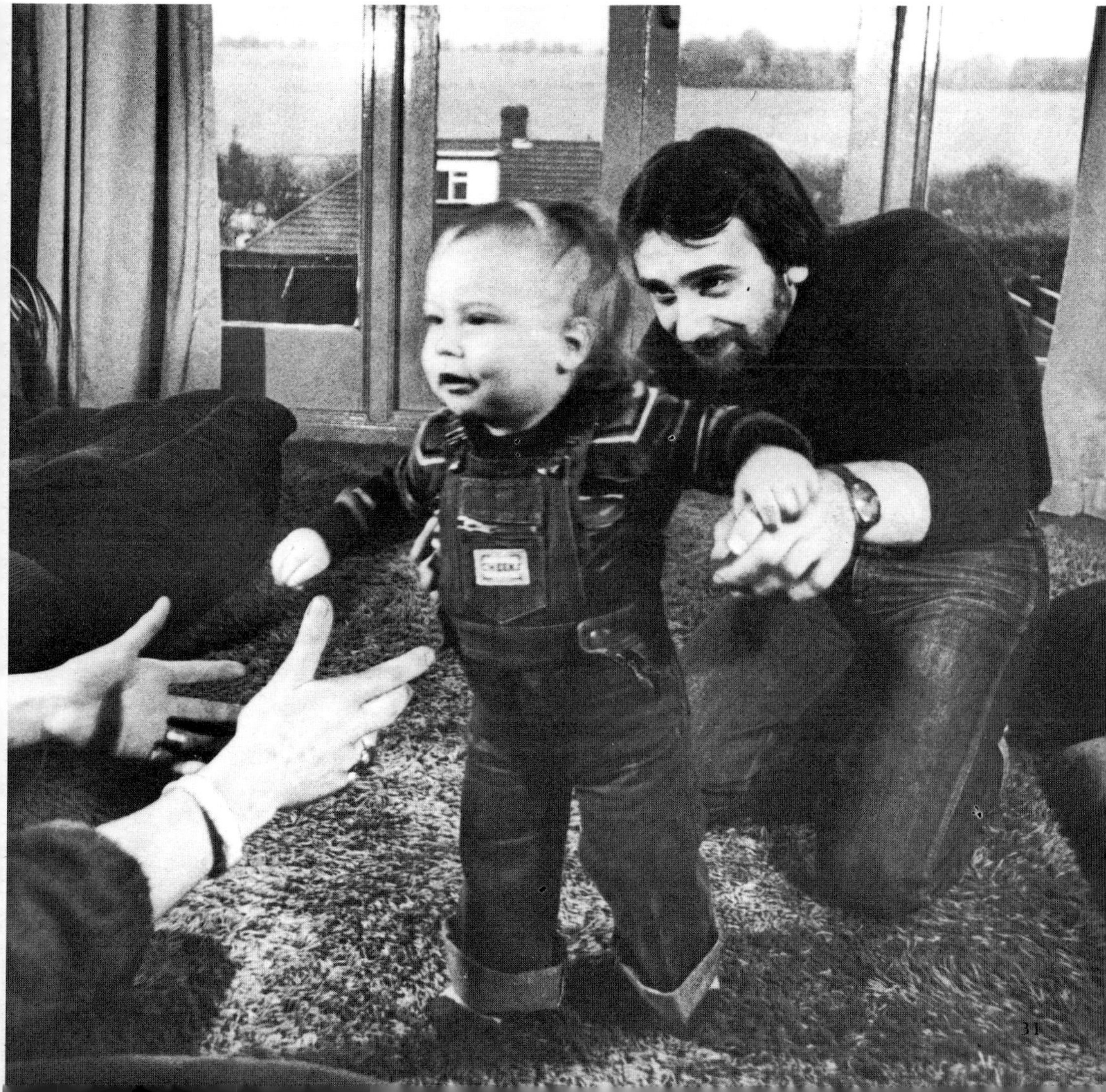

# Development from one to two years

Walking is a technique which is acquired at any time between one year and eighteen months. The majority of children will be able to walk, holding on to pieces of furniture, at between twelve and thirteen months. Walking without support is usually achieved at between thirteen and fourteen months. Some children, for example those of African origin, will walk earlier – some may even do so at ten months.

Initially, the infant's gait will be faltering and his legs will be rather wide apart to assist the shaky balance. He will often fall to begin with, nearly always sitting down rather sharply. As his legs are much shorter than his body at this age he will not have too far to fall, and the only pain sustained

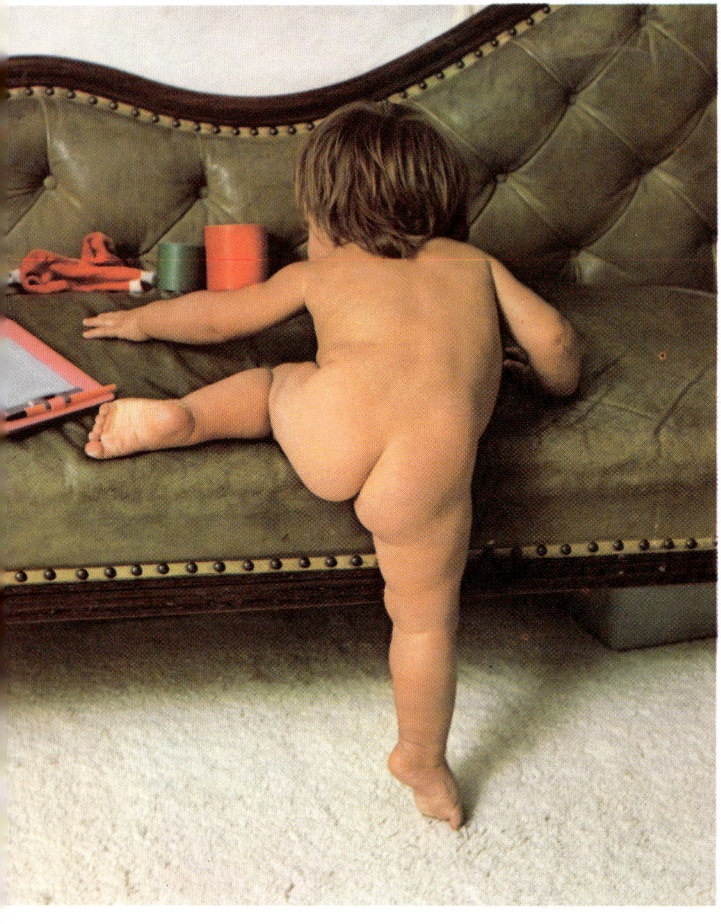

▶ Children of fifteen months who can already walk without support will enjoy pushing a small trolley around the house. When filled with toys, trolleys have the advantage of giving the child some stability in awkward situations.

◀ At two years, and often slightly younger, the child will enjoy climbing on to low pieces of furniture, especially to reach objects which have been put there to be out of his way.

will be to his dignity. Gaits will vary at this early stage. Variations include slight trailing of one leg or walking with feet turned outwards. The latter is very common nowadays and is probably related to the custom of nursing newborn babies on their abdomens. It is especially evident in children who were born prematurely. It is not normal for a child to begin walking on the ball of the foot: the gait should be flat-footed at this stage. Typically, the child will have a slightly lowered gaze during early walking, giving little attention to objects above eye level. This may cause him to bump his head on pieces of furniture, especially dining-tables, unless the way is cleared for him.

It is interesting to notice that children of one to two years of age will react to laughter with displeasure if the laughter is directed *at* them rather than shared *with* them.

**Age fifteen months** The child will be much more sure-footed by now, provided he started walking at the usual time. He will manage a cup well with both hands, lifting it to his mouth and replacing it after drinking. It is only to be expected that he will spill a considerable amount!

He will also use a spoon to convey food to his mouth, grasping it with the four fingers of the hand at right angles to the handle and the thumb underneath. He will tend to rotate the spoon just before inserting it into the mouth, causing some spillage. It is important not to give a young child a spoon with a long handle, as these are much more difficult for him to control. A short spoon with a good-sized bowl is the most satisfactory.

From nine months onwards, most babies 'drool'. Almost universal, this habit seems to coincide with the arrival of teeth; by fifteen months, it will have more or less stopped.

The pincer grasp should be perfectly developed by now and the child will show considerable ability in picking up even very small objects. Chewing should provide no problems by now, providing the food is cut into small and manageable pieces.

At about this age the child will attempt to crawl up stairs, as long as they are not too steep.

**Age eighteen months** The child will now walk well and with considerable confidence, provided he began walking at the usual time (thirteen to fourteen months). He will enjoy propelling himself towards all manner of desired objects. His parents will now have to anticipate his ability to reach undesirable or dangerous objects such as domestic cleaning solutions or the bars of an electric fire. Whenever possible, dangerous items should be locked up or put well out of reach.

The child will be able, by now, to back himself on to a small chair without any anxiety. Although he may use either hand for some manipulations he will prefer to use one hand in particular for others. This will be particularly noticeable where feeding with a spoon is concerned. (Exclusive use of one hand for most tasks develops much later and is abnormal at this age.) If given a pencil, he will grasp it in his fist, pressing it firmly on a sheet of paper and making side-to-side movements. He will almost invariably use his preferred hand for this activity. Similarly, he will use the same hand consistently for throwing a small ball. His co-ordination will now be good enough for him to balance three small bricks on top of each other, providing he is shown how to first. He will drink from a cup much more surely now, spilling very little.

Although frequently very demanding of time and attention, the child of eighteen months will bring his parents many rewards. He will enjoy imitating his mother's domestic activities, such as dusting, and will be content to be diverted in this way. Even more gratifying will be his tendency to indicate the need for a potty *before* actually defecating. His ability to communicate verbally will have advanced considerably since the age of twelve months, and he will use up to twenty recognizable words. Some children of this age use only three or four, and none is likely to use two words at a time yet. Speech development varies considerably from infant to infant and parents should not be worried if their child can say only a few words at this age. Failure to use any recognizable words at this age is abnormal and suggests difficulty in hearing. However, if the child is capable of obeying simple commands, he can both hear *and* understand. He should now be able, on request, to indentify the nose, eyes and mouth of his mother by touching them.

**Age two years** He will now walk completely automatically and with excellent

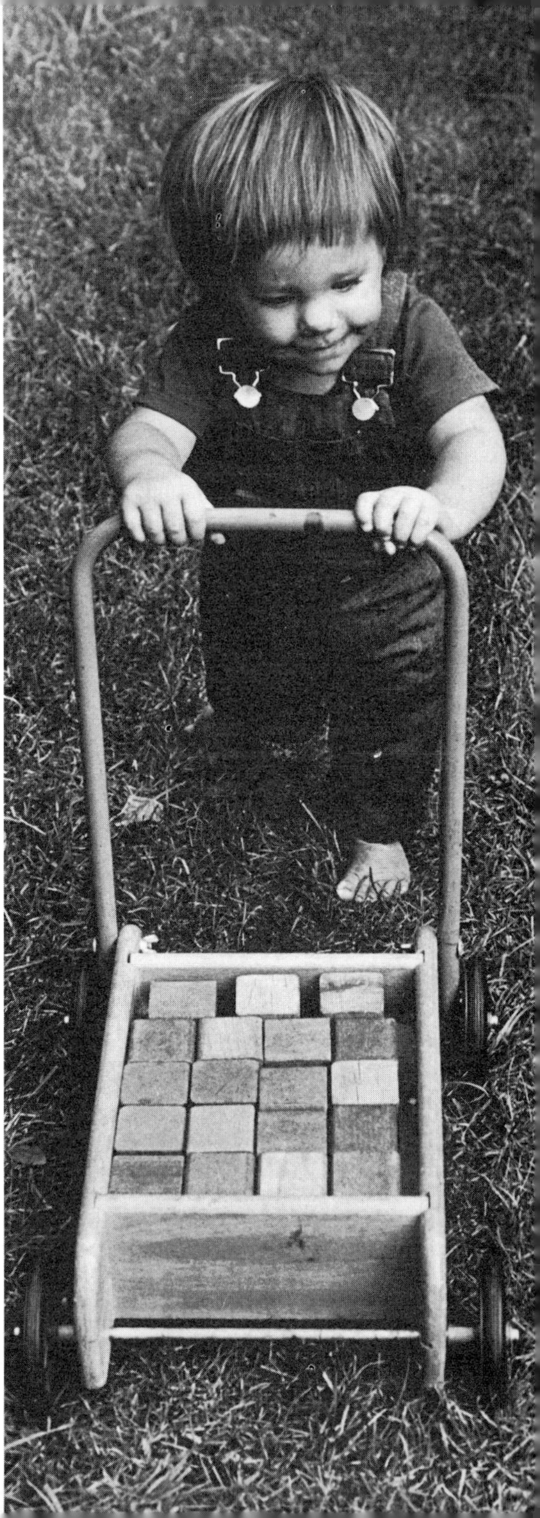

co-ordination. He will be expert at getting around the house and may climb on and off the furniture in a way which will surprise his parents. He may get into predicaments which frighten him (and his mother) at times, especially when he climbs on to something from which he is unable to get down. His balance will be good and for three or four months he will have been able to bend down to pick objects off the floor without holding on for support.

He will be able to walk backwards for several steps without overbalancing and to jump off a small step without fear. Walking, as opposed to crawling, up stairs will start at about twenty months, and will be achieved by holding on to the banister and leading with the dominant foot. The other foot will be brought alongside and the process repeated. Alternating steps, in which the left and right feet are used to ascend, are not used until very much later. By two years he should be able to walk down stairs although he will tend to be rather cautious about this. He will also be able to run quite well using a trotting motion but will have difficulty in pulling up sharply. He will enjoy trying to kick a ball and will be able to do this without overbalancing.

He will now usually insist on feeding himself, and will use a spoon quite competently. He will also drink from a cup, lifting and replacing it without spilling. Competence at feeding himself will naturally depend on practice. It is better to resist the temptation to feed the child yourself to avoid mess, because at this age he should be allowed to experiment. Similarly, laziness may encourage some mothers to hand their child a feeding bottle rather than taking the extra time necessary for getting him used to a cup.

By two years, many children have bladder control by day. In other words, the child will indicate that he needs to pass

◀ By two years, the child will be sure-footed and will no longer need a trolley to give him stability. He will instead use the trolley as a means of transporting objects over often considerable distances and may sometimes do this on the run.

▶ Between eighteen months and two years, the child's curiosity will be boundless and nothing within reach can be considered safe from his attentions. Breakable or potentially dangerous items should never be kept in ground-level cupboards. Poisonous substances should be kept in locked cupboards.

urine by asking for his pot or pulling down his trousers. He will not, however, be dry at night.

Although the child will not be able to dress himself in any way he will be able to remove certain articles of clothing, such as socks and shoes. He will be able to put on a simple hat if he normally wears one.

His vocabulary will have increased to more than fifty words and he will put two or more words together to make a rudimentary sentence. There will be many difficulties in pronunciation. This is normal, and zealous attempts to correct errors will not result in improvement: speech control develops with the passage of time and constant correction may cause stuttering when the child is older.

He will enjoy a book with pictures and will like to turn the pages for himself,

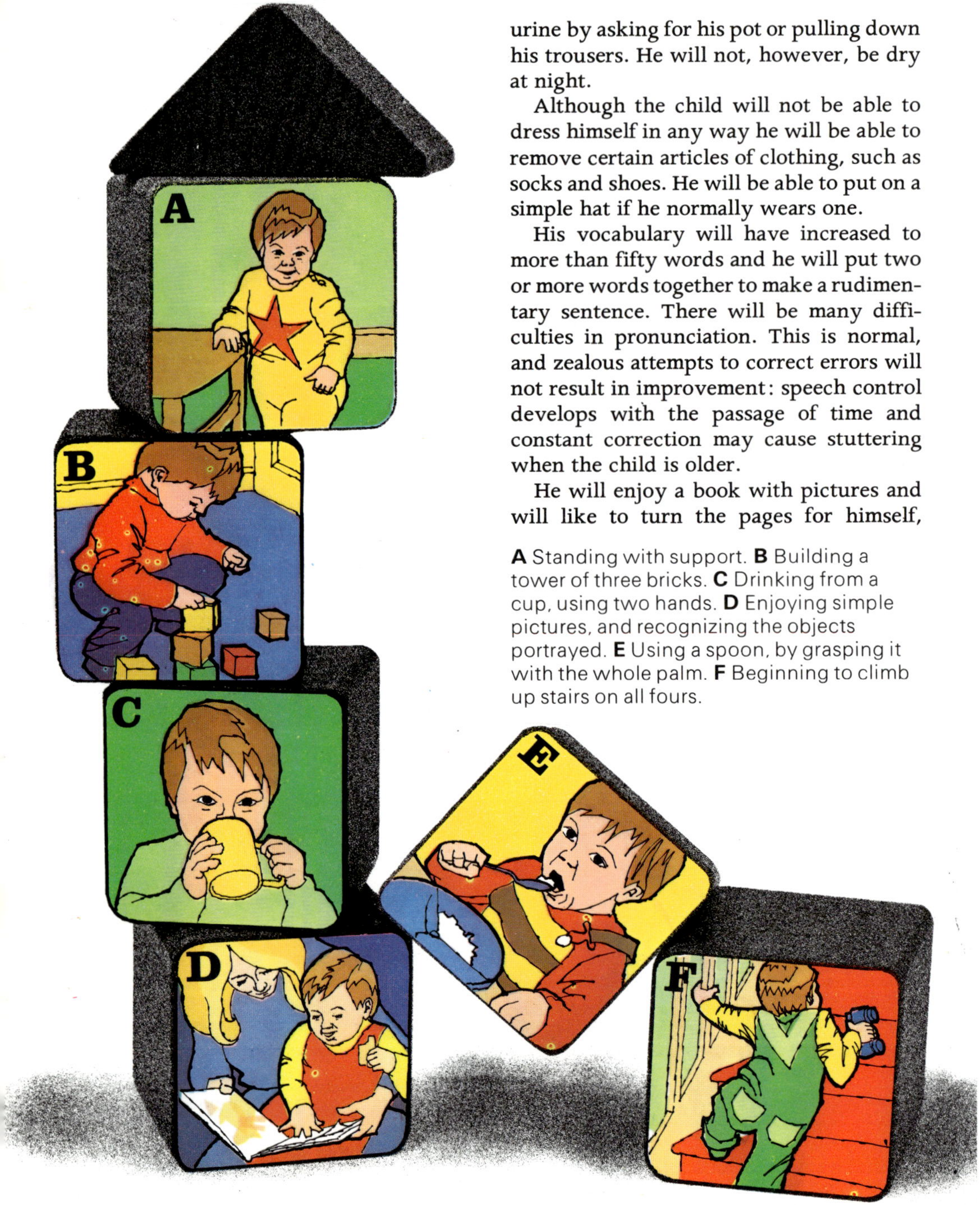


**A** Standing with support. **B** Building a tower of three bricks. **C** Drinking from a cup, using two hands. **D** Enjoying simple pictures, and recognizing the objects portrayed. **E** Using a spoon, by grasping it with the whole palm. **F** Beginning to climb up stairs on all fours.

vocalizing freely as he does so. He will build a tower of five or six bricks and enjoy knocking it down once he has built it.

Many children of two years enjoy playing with small objects; toy cars are a special favourite. The child will now play more independently and be contented to play on his own without adult participation. He will prefer playing with an adult near at hand, and will talk to himself happily. Any object which he can easily grasp and manipulate will absorb his attention. He will particularly enjoy putting objects in small containers. At this age children tend to play alongside others rather than with them. Company is shared but activities are not.

## Psycho-sexual drives

It is broadly accepted that sexuality in the adult sense has its roots in earliest infancy. This view enraged the public at the time when the hypothesis was first put forward by the Viennese doctor Sigmund Freud in the early years of the twentieth century. His views were largely misunderstood at that time because people naively translated their own concept of sexuality to Freud's theories as applied to young infants. They objected strongly to what they imagined was the idea that innocent babies harboured lustful thoughts! Needless to say, this was far from what Freud intended. Basically, he believed that the fully developed sexual drive of the adult does not arise suddenly and inexplicably at the time that pubic hair appears. He argued from simple observation that the basic drive is present from birth but takes a different form during different phases of childhood.

Freud maintained that at different ages during childhood this drive expresses itself by preoccupation with and pleasure in certain areas of the body. In the early months, the centre of pleasure is the mouth. The drive to locate the maternal nipple and to suck upon it at birth has survival value – a concept which is less easy to recognize in developed societies but crucial in primitive ones. In primitive tribes, the child who cannot suck at the breast will die. The element of pleasure obtained by sucking on the breast can be seen to be more than just the satiation of hunger. The relaxation and appearance of blissful pleasure noted by mothers will convince most sceptics.

This 'oral phase' will become increasingly obvious by six months of age, when objects placed in the child's hands are not held up for inspection or manipulated for the appreciation of their textural quality, but are taken directly to the mouth and explored with the tongue.

The predominance of the mouth as an 'erogenous zone' diminishes steadily from one to two years, when the anus becomes the most important area of sensation. Children of between two and three years (when problems relating to toilet-training frequently arise), enjoy fingering the anus. Later, usually between four and five years, the erogenous zone is fixed around the genitalia.

Many psychoanalysts have speculated about the effects of parental interference with these stages of sexual interest, and generally agree that interference can only make matters worse. The effects of attempting to toilet-train an infant according to strict rules have been specifically investigated. Such training is said by some experts to produce in later life a so-called anal-fixated personality, whose main characteristics are obsession with details and tidiness and resistance to external pressures amounting to extreme obstinacy. It is generally considered that the exact time a child chooses to use a pot is not crucial, though it is likely to be between two and four years.

# Separations of mother and child

It is not generally realized that sudden and unexpected separations of mother and child, even for as little as a week, can sometimes have adverse effects on children. This is especially true for children of between one and three years. A child of this age cannot understand why he should be parted from his mother (for example, if she is admitted to hospital), and even if he did understand the implications, he would still be anxious and probably miserable. If the period of separation is considerable, the ultimate reunion may be difficult. Often, behaviour problems will occur as a result, requiring a great deal of patience and understanding from parents. Some children are much more disturbed by separations than others and it is not possible to predict in advance whether a child will be seriously affected. The particular vulnerability of pre-school-age children to being parted from their mothers needs to be borne in mind before any such action is contemplated. Sometimes separation will be unavoidable; on some occasions, however, there may be an alternative.

▼ Even when mother is away, the child can remain in contact by telephone, with father's help.

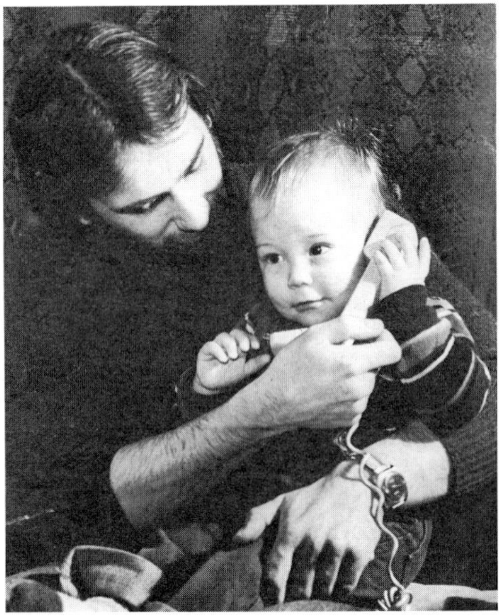

**Hospitalization of the child** If a young child falls prey to some acute illness, hospitalization will be the usual solution. However, this is by no means always the case. Many acute admissions to hospital are determined not only by the degree of illness in the child but also by the hospital doctor's assessment of the mother's capacity to cope at home. He will try to assess the family's circumstances: the housing conditions, the emotional and practical support available and of course the desire and ability of the mother to look after the child at home. Sometimes, particularly in the evening and if the child is seen by a less experienced doctor, in-patient care may be recommended because the doctor will feel more in control of the case once the child has undergone overnight observation. Frequently, the child will be discharged the following day on the advice of a more senior doctor. This problem is common in inner cities, where the general practitioner service may leave a lot to be desired; in such circumstances, mothers tend to take their children directly to a hospital casualty department. If, however, the general practitioner is trusted and conscientious, and has prior knowledge of the family and the child, unnecessary admission to hospital can be avoided. It is wise, therefore, to contact the family doctor first whenever

▲ Relatives may fulfil a vital role when parents and young children are unavoidably separated for a while.

possible, as he will be in the best position to decide whether hospital care as opposed to home care is desirable. If you take a child directly to a casualty department, it is worth asking the hospital doctor whether you can look after the child at home. Often, this will be allowed, providing you agree to have the child seen by the family doctor in the morning.

Young children are usually bewildered and afraid when taken into hospital. They may think they are being abandoned or even punished. The typical children's ward is noisy, lacking the air of calm and discipline found in adult wards. This may be the first time that the child has been exposed to so many other children, all of different ages, and to so many unfamiliar adults. As the child is likely to be unwell also, he may find it a very intimidating experience. His initial reaction will usually be to accept this without vigorous protest until the time comes for his parents to leave, when he will cry. This is quite normal, although parents, obviously, are likely to find it distressing. If the in-patient stay is prolonged, the child may stop protesting and crying and lapse into apathy. During this stage he may smile very little and display little interest in his surroundings. Later he may seem to recover, accepting all that happens and showing friendliness to all comers indiscriminately. The stages of apathy and apparent recovery are warnings that the child is giving up the struggle for individuality and is becoming institutionalized.

When he returns home, problems may occur, including incessant clinging to the mother, fear of being left alone in a room

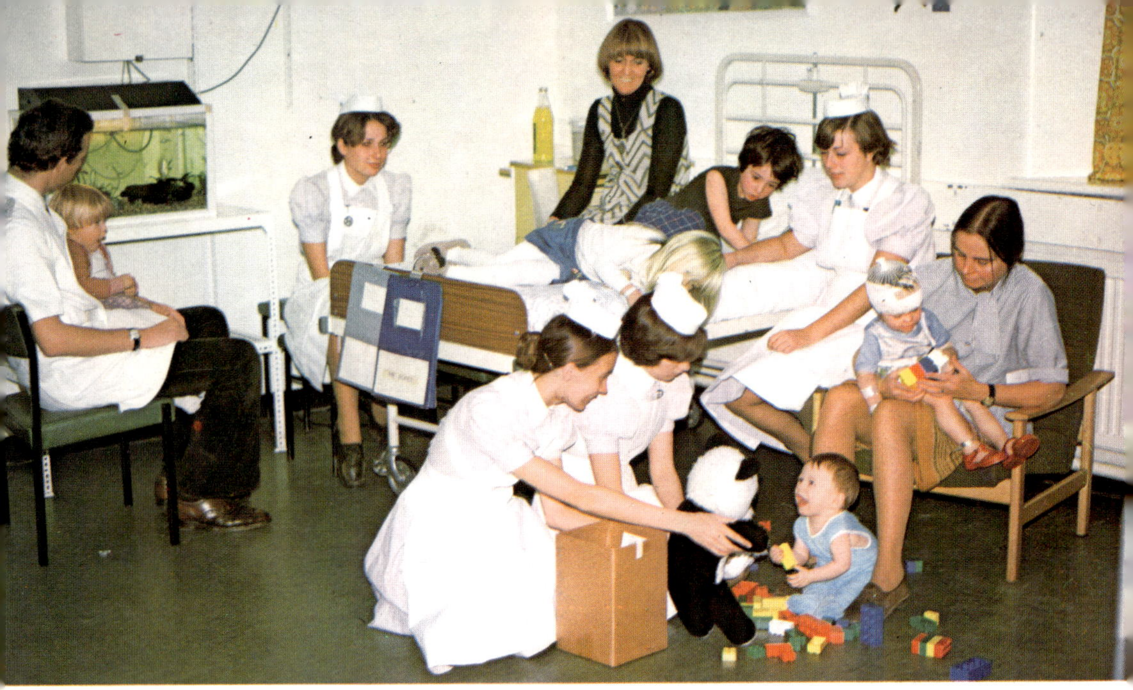

for a few moments, nightmares, difficulty in sleeping, tantrums, poor appetite and difficulty in adapting to the company of other children. He will usually show signs of fear when taken to hospital for his outpatient follow-up appointment and will be difficult to examine. Visits to the family doctor for subsequent illnesses may present further problems.

Fortunately, these warning signs are easily recognized for what they are by the nurses and doctors and can be prevented before they occur. Unrestricted visiting is now the rule in children's wards and when combined with a more enlightened approach to freedom within the ward itself, hospitals are far less frightening places for children. Many hospitals have accommodation for mothers, which any anxious mother can request. Although priority is given to nursing mothers and to those who live far away, most hospitals will make every effort to accommodate those who ask. It is of great importance for parents to spend as much time as they can spare with their child if he has to stay in hospital during his early years. This is invaluable both for the child and for those who are looking after him. The mother should not feel diffident about being present when the doctors come to see her child; today, most doctors prefer this. Free visiting means the mother can visit whenever and for as long as she wishes, and talk with the ward sister on an informal basis. It is also a valuable safety valve for her emotions.

Most hospitals like to discharge children as soon as they can be looked after at home, as long as the mother feels she can cope with a convalescent child.

**Hospitalization of the mother** Often, this happens because she is giving birth to another child. If the firstborn is unaware of the impending separation he may feel a considerable sense of loss. Although most mothers will have explained to their child

◀ Being in hospital can be more pleasant for a child than parents might imagine. Children's nurses try to spend spare moments talking and playing with their patients.
▼ The presence of the mother during the doctor's rounds will help him when he wishes to examine a small patient.

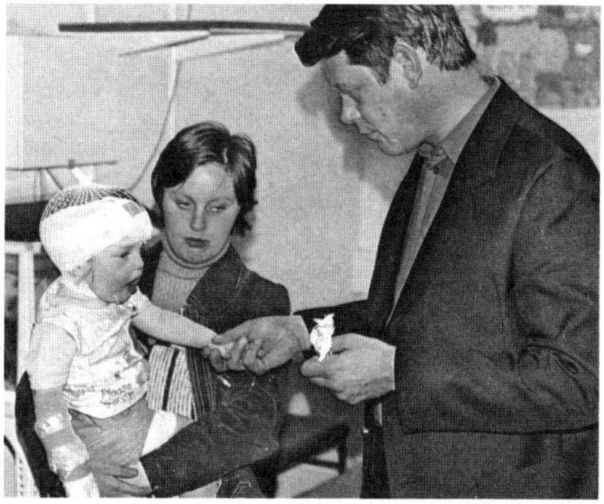

that a new baby is coming, some will forget to explain that this may involve a short separation. On the whole it is desirable for the firstborn to remain at home while the mother is in hospital. This may mean that his father takes time off work or that his grandparents move in for a while to look after him. Although it may be convenient to place the child at the home of neighbours or relatives, it is undesirable to combine the separation with a change of environment. The child will feel rather left out in any case, without being taken away from his own home. When the new baby is born, the other child should be taken to visit his mother and to see the baby. This will give him an immediate sense of involvement and remove the sensation of mystery which often surrounds the event. The child's father can be a great help here, making him feel as valued as ever and diminishing his natural feelings of jealousy.

If the reason for mother's hospital admission is illness, this should be explained as fully as he is capable of understanding. Secretiveness and anxious whispering sometimes generate great fear, which is made worse by failure to explain.

**Temporary fostering** Sometimes, as when the mother has no partner, married or otherwise, it may be necessary for her child to be fostered. If such action is necessary – and it should not be taken unless there is absolutely no alternative – it will usually be arranged by local authority social workers. In some cases, mothers have children fostered while they attend courses in higher education establishments, but fostering is a very drastic step to take for such a reason and suggests a misguided sense of priorities in the mother. Almost all educational institutions will permit an interruption of studies until more suitable arrangements can be made for the child.

**Child minders** These women look after children during normal working hours in return for a fee. It is important to check that the child minder you choose is registered with the local authority, which means that she has supplied suitable references and her premises have been inspected by the health and fire-prevention authorities.

Beware of using unregistered child minders, who are operating illegally. Some of these are highly unsuitable and have no conception of the emotional needs of young children. Some unregistered minders will look after a child for a whole working week, both day and night. They usually perform this service for young, unsupported mothers. However, separation of mother and child for five days at a time, on a regular basis, is highly undesirable. The life style is extremely confusing for the child and is never justifiable. Moreover, it may lead to severe behaviour problems in the child, such as tantrums and screaming attacks at night.

# Development from two to five years

**Age two years** The child will now be steadily outgrowing many of the characteristics of the baby period. The necessity of watching the child constantly when he is physically active will progressively decrease. His co-operation will become much more certain and the need to protect him from injuring himself will therefore lessen. He will enjoy running and jumping for its own sake and begin to appreciate boisterous play, but although his physical independence will be increasing, his emotional dependence and demands will be considerable. By now, he will not usually mind being left in a room on his own for short periods, but he will not like being left to his own devices in unfamiliar surroundings for more than five or ten minutes. He will by now thoroughly enjoy helping mother with her housework, using his own little dustpan and brush.

His speech will now be much more sophisticated. As his sphere of activities widens, his desires will become more complicated, therefore his speech will need to progress in order to express them. His facial

▼ Between four and five years, many children enjoy riding tricycles, or bicycles with stabilizers fitted.

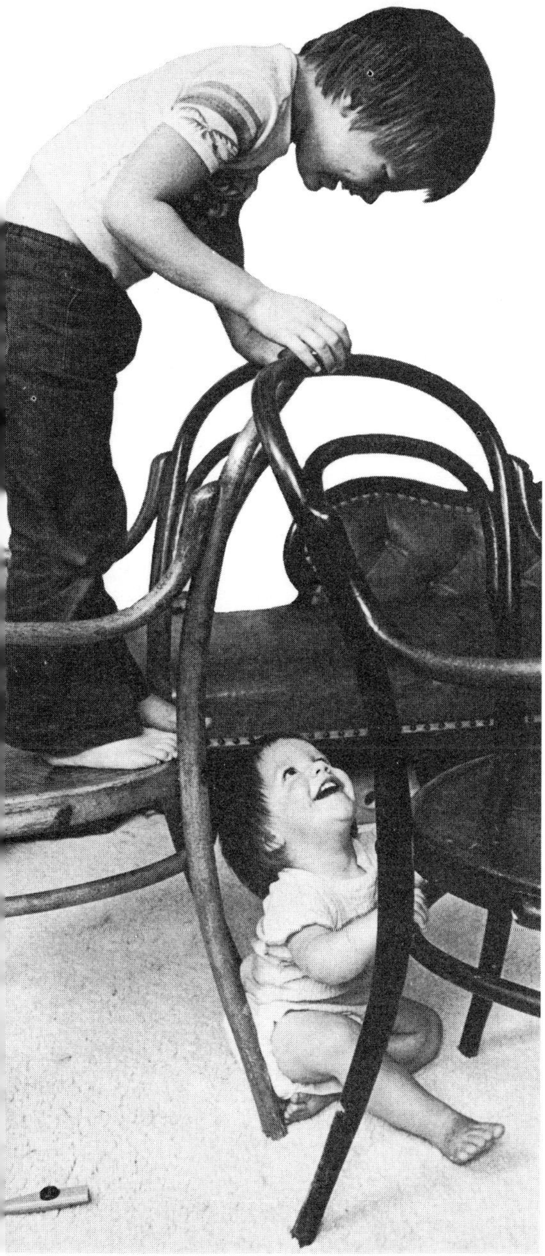

▲ Toddlers greatly enjoy boisterous play, but if play between a young child and his elder brother or sister becomes too rough, the younger child may become frightened.

expressions and gestures will become increasingly more appropriate to individual situations. He will also tend to chatter endlessly when playing.

**Age three years** By now his co-ordination should be good enough to allow him to balance on either foot alone. He will be able to run easily without falling and to manoeuvre himself around objects scattered about the floor. His ability to stop quickly when running will be well developed. He will enjoy throwing and kicking a ball; if it is large, he may attempt to catch it when it is thrown to him, and will occasionally be successful.

Fine movements will also be much better controlled. Most children of this age will be able to copy a circle if shown how to do so. Some will be able to do this without a demonstration by the parent when shown a completed circle. Most will also be able to build a tower of nine bricks, even if the bricks are only small. The average three-year-old will be able to use a fork as well as a spoon but will not be able to use a knife for cutting up food. He will be competent at undressing, provided difficult buttons and buckles are undone for him, and will frequently be able to manage an accessible zip fastener.

The child's vocabulary at this age is usually considerable but many sounds will be mispronounced. People who do not know the child well may have difficulty in understanding his speech, while his mother will usually comprehend most of it. The speech of many children at this age is generally unintelligible; constant correction, apart from being unhelpful, may lead to speech defects such as stammering.

**Age four years** The child's sense of balance will be sufficiently developed for him to hop up to six times on one foot. He will run swiftly and surely with a less flatfooted gait than that seen in three-year-olds. He will also be able to walk along a straight line, heel to toe, without overbalancing. Many three-year-olds will invariably walk up stairs in the adult fashion: that is, taking alternating steps rather than always advancing with the same foot and bringing the other up to it. Some children do not manage this until they are four.

Almost all children will now be completely dry and clean by day, but may not necessarily be dry at night. However, if a child who has been consistently dry at night at three years starts wetting regularly at four, he may be suffering from acute anxiety or even be emotionally disturbed. Emotional disturbance is an even stronger likelihood if a child who was clean by day at the usual time (two years) starts soiling again when he is older. Some significant emotional upheaval is implicated if the wetting – or soiling – continues for more than a month. Temporary soiling, usually following a diarrhoeal illness, may occur for ten days or so, but seldom longer. Regular soiling at four years should be dealt with by a doctor: without medical attention, the condition seldom improves.

The child's ability to dress and undress without assistance will now be well developed. He will be able to undo and do up all his buttons, providing they are situated within his range of vision. He will have difficulty with very small buttons and he may still have difficulty in buckling sandals, which have small buckles, though he can manage belts.

His speech will probably be completely intelligible to people who do not know him. Some children, however, speak with a lalling intonation which may be difficult for some, especially the elderly, to hear (advancing age can cause deterioration in the ability to hear sounds of higher frequency, such as a child's piping speech tones). Most four-year-olds pronounce consonants quite clearly and make few infantile substitutions of consonants. (The most common example of the latter is to use 'f' for 'th', as in 'forty fousand fevvers on a frush'.) All children of this age should be able to give their full name and address; advanced children will also know their telephone number.

The average four-year-old can name colours (up to four in number) and when playing with bricks will be able to copy a model of stairs with six or more cubes.

He will enjoy playing *with* children of his own age rather than alongside them. He may also be able to accept the idea of taking turns without getting into a rage.

**Age five years** By now constant vigilance while the child is physically active will have long ceased to be necessary. He will skip from foot to foot and enjoy climbing whenever the opportunity arises. Instead of kicking a ball from a static position as he did at four years, he will have no difficulty in delivering a running kick. He will find going down stairs is more difficult than ascending, and only now will he begin to descend using alternating steps. He will climb in and out of a car, or on to a bus, without difficulty or fear.

His use of writing implements will now be much more mature. He will be able to copy a square as well as a circle and a cross, but not a diamond.

His speech will be fluent, and he will be able to express simple abstract ideas. He will substitute incorrect consonants only occasionally. He will be able to count up to five objects at a time and will know his birth date.

He will prefer to dress and undress without help, unless very tired, and will resent attempts to cut up food for him.

The concept of games with rules will now be acceptable to him and attempts by others to cheat will aggrieve him. He will prefer to pick and choose his own friends and will be

**A** Using fork and spoon—grasping with the whole palm. **B** Copying a circle, after a demonstration. **C** Increased coordination makes hopping possible. **D** Recognizing and naming familiar objects. **E** Attempting to undress unaided. **F** Washing the face.

interested in communal play. He will want to try riding a bicycle but will not manage unless stabilizers have been fitted. He will soon be ready for school and will look forward to this if he has had previous experience of nursery school or a play-group. If a child of five finds it difficult to socialize, it will usually be because he has not mixed much with other children rather than because he is innately timid.

With the advent of formal schooling a whole new world will be opened up to the child and his need for independence at home will increase.

# Behaviour problems from two to five years

The term 'behaviour problem' will mean different things to different people. Most mothers know some other mother whose children seem to be 'impossible': dictatorial, aggressive, negativistic and bloody-minded. They will be amazed at this mother's casual acceptance of such behaviour on the part of her offspring as kicking other children or smashing one household item after another. Yet if one of their children should 'playfully' smack another child in the face, his mother will be amazed at the resulting parental indignation! What is acceptable in one family is therefore not necessarily acceptable in another. The upbringing of different parents and therefore their expectations regarding their own children's behaviour will vary a great deal, too. Some parents, perhaps the products of a very strict upbringing, are too demanding and have little insight into what can be expected of the young child. The 'behaviour problem' of their child may be non-existent, the real problem being their unrealistic attitudes.

## Jealousy

One of the earliest problems may occur when a new baby is born, in the form of jealousy on the part of the child who was previously the youngest of the family. He will probably reveal his jealousy by drawing attention to himself whenever possible, by being unco-operative or by bursting into fits of temper frequently. This is particularly likely if he is between two and three years, because such a phase is characteristic of this age group in any case. It is quite normal and understandable that this type of behaviour should be accentuated when a new baby arrives in the home. The situation can be helped a great deal by demonstrating to the older child that the needs of the baby do not invariably override his own. It is also helpful if the mother can devote several short periods a day to him alone – for example, when the baby is sleeping. As newborn babies sleep up to sixteen hours a day, this should not prove too difficult to arrange. Outbursts of hostility on the part of the older child towards the newcomer are usually transitory and easily diverted. Some children accept a new baby with apparent equanimity, but such tolerance always has its ambivalent aspects and extra attention should still be given to the older child even if he does not appear to demand it.

Sometimes normal jealousy may become pathological. If the older child studiously ignores the newcomer at all times, or attemps to hit his new brother or sister at every available opportunity, if he starts constantly clinging to the mother, crying incessantly at night, refuses to eat or becomes completely apathetic, severe disturbance is indicated and informed medical advice should be sought.

## Breath-holding attacks

Sometimes children hold their breath following minor injury or during the course of a tantrum. The breath-holding may last until the child's lips turn blue and he may even become unconscious for a few seconds. Although it is alarming to watch a child do this, parents should realize that no one can hold their breath until they die. The child will start breathing again within a very short time and return completely to normal in a few seconds. Breath-holding is really an extreme form of tantrum and does not need medical attention if it is a relatively infrequent occurrence. If such outbursts occur daily, however, paediatric advice should be sought.

## Autism

This is fortunately a rare condition, the cause of which is unknown. It is characterized by extreme lack of responsiveness to any affection and to people in general. Autistic children are completely withdrawn; they ignore and avoid the gaze of those around them. Concepts of right and wrong do not exist for autistics and they have great difficulty in learning to speak. Their intelligence is often, but not always sub-normal. Special psychiatric treatment can help them.

## Soiling and bed-wetting

As mentioned in the previous chapter, the child who starts soiling himself after previously having been clean is usually disturbed. The roots of the problem will lie within the family, and while medical treatment will be useless, child psychiatry will be very helpful. Bed-wetting is a family problem. As ten per cent of normal five-year-olds are not dry at night, patience rather than medicine is needed.

## Masturbation

In children this is not true masturbation with orgasm but playing with the genitalia with the fingers. Small boys often enjoy holding their penises when in bed or in the bath, or when playing. The habit is completely normal and harmless. It should not be discouraged or commented upon unless taken to extremes.

## Hyperactivity

Many children are described as 'hyperactive' by their parents, usually with the implication that the child is constantly 'on the go'. In fact, even very active children will rest for a few minutes at times or play intently with a toy on occasion. True hyperactivity is usually caused by either a very disturbed and unsettled family environment or by a minor degree of brain damage in the child. A hyperactive child can be recognized by his constant and frequently purposeless rushing around without a break. His behaviour is never modified by the presence of strangers or a visit to the doctor, unlike that of the active but otherwise normal child. The hyperactive child's span of attention is extremely short and he will find constructive play of any kind is impossible. Such children are frequently very clumsy; this characteristic, allied to a strong distractibility, may result in many breakages. The hyperactive child sleeps for only short periods and exhausts and depresses his parents. If hyperactivity is suspected in a child, he should be seen by a paediatrician at once, for this is an intractable problem which often causes marital breakdown and violence in parents.

## Head banging and rocking

This curious habit is fortunately not common but can be very worrying for mothers. The child will sit in his cot, rocking to and fro and simultaneously banging his head against the bars, sometimes quite forcefully. Mothers are usually concerned that the child will damage his head. Fortunately this happens on extremely rare occasions, although bruises do occur from time to time. The real cause for concern should be the underlying reason for the habit, which is most usually found in disturbed or emotionally deprived infants, institutionalized children, the mentally retarded and the autistic, rather than in children who come from a loving home. Head banging may herald the beginning of an emotional rift between mother and child. For this reason, expert advice is desirable. More cuddling and attempts to divert the child will certainly be helpful.

Like head banging, rocking is a way in which the child comforts himself when other stimulation is lacking. It is not very important if it only lasts for a minute or two but if it is more or less continuous expert advice should be obtained.

## Nail-biting

This is a habit, not a sign of emotional trouble. Although unsightly, it is harmless. Apart from occasional comment it should not be prevented. Attempts to do so may induce much more undesirable tendencies.

## Thumb-sucking

This is also harmless but may be extremely comforting to the child. It tends to run in families and is extremely rare after puberty. The child will cease thumb-sucking in his own good time. In any case, it is impossible to prevent the habit.

## Cruelty to animals

In young children this rarely stems from malice. Thoughtlessness is a more likely cause. Cruelty to animals usually takes the form of physical experimentation, such as pulling a cat's tail to assess its response. As the response will usually be swift – and painful for the child – he will rapidly learn from the experience!

At four years and over, the child should be aware that certain treatment is unpleasant for animals and that he should refrain from it. Children who are never checked from behaving in a manner which is unpleasant to other people are more likely to behave in an unfeeling way towards animals. A child needs to be made aware that animals do not exist for his sole gratification: showing obvious disapproval or removing the child from the animal will usually suffice. Persistent maltreatment of an animal, particularly if the child finds it pleasurable, is an ominous sign, and it is unlikely that he will be emotionally normal in other spheres. Child guidance from a child psychiatrist is essential in such a situation.

## Treatment of behaviour problems

Behaviour causing grave parental concern may occur because of a basic deficiency in the relationship between them and their child. The advice of a paediatrician is essential; he will refer the child to a child psychiatrist if necessary. Often, parents' expectations of what they believe to be 'normal' behaviour are unrealistic, and there will be no need for further consultation.

# Speech development

▲ Young children learn to acquire speech from their parents. Even when the child is too young to understand, it is important to talk to him.

The development of language is a sophisticated process which depends upon intact hearing and is helped by vision. Apart from crying, the new-born infant does not vocalize in the accepted sense. As he gets older he can see his mother's mouth moving as she talks to him. He is capable of responding to the human voice even in the first week of life.

**Age two months** He will already be able to distinguish soothing or loving noises from unpleasant sounds or angry voices. He will respond to the former by little murmurs and cooing sounds and to the latter by looking worried or crying.

**Age three months** He will now be making a variety of different noises when he is contented, and is in fact experimenting with his new skill. The mother can rarely resist imitating his new noises, interspersing her mimicry with a mixture of normal speech and other, often meaningless, sounds.

This interplay between mother and child is very important as it encourages the infant to use his voice and to respond vocally. Deaf children will also vocalize but the interplay with the mother will be lacking and the range of vocal expression limited. Infants who are emotionally deprived and rarely spoken to will be less vocal and generally more apathetic than those with attentive parents.

**Age six months** The infant will by now make predictable noises in certain situations. Most of these noises will be sounds involving lip movement – the so-called labial sounds. He will have discovered the technique of vibrating his lips with his fingers while vocalizing. The most common noise he makes will probably be 'mum-mum', although this does not in fact have meaning at this time. The origin of the word 'mum' probably relates to these first labial sounds as it tends to be fairly constant whatever the culture.

**Age one year** By now, the word 'mum' will apply more specifically to the mother and the use of gestures is becoming part of communication. Good hearing is all-important, because new words are acquired by mimicry, with their appropriate usage being acquired later. New words are learnt from those closest to the child and often used indiscriminately. The joining of two words together occurs between eighteen months and two years. The words are usually nouns, including proper names, with verbs being used rarely.

**Age two years** Many children of this age use up to fifty words with meaning. Some speech at this age will be relatively unintelligible to strangers, but the child's family will recognize his jargon and gestures without difficulty. It is important to talk to the child as often as possible at this time, for language development strongly depends upon hearing meaningful speech. The child will then practise these sounds on other listeners.

By two and a half years the child will make noticeable use of the past tense, as well as plurals. He will use three-word sentences frequently and his vocabulary will have progressed considerably.

**Age three years** He will be chattering a great deal by now, especially when playing alone. He will tell little stories about his experiences and express his fantasies vocally. He will use much less jargon: that is, made-up words which have special meaning for him. He will enjoy little conversations with adults.

**Age four years** Four-year-olds vary widely in their speech abilities. Many at this age will still make infantile substitutions for certain consonants while others will be extremely fluent.

**Age five years** The child should now be able to name all the colours. He will become interested in words themselves and ask their meaning. Many children will be able to print their own name, writing being an extension of the language process.

## Delay in talking

Parents may become worried if, by the age of two, their child is using only two or three words interspersed with unintelligible jargon. Usually there is nothing wrong at all, as the rate of speech development varies widely. If the child understands simple commands such as 'Shut the door' or 'Bring Mummy the ball' given in a normal conversational tone, and if he then obeys them, he is capable of both hearing and understanding. It is important to establish this, because deafness and mental backwardness are the two most common abnormal causes of delayed speech.

Some children between two and three years find they can get what they want by a combination of gesture, facial expression or pointing, without resorting to intelligible speech, so they do not concern themselves with the latter. Exceptionally, some children may not speak until four years, as in the case of the late Sir Winston Churchill.

Children under three are given speech therapy only if they have hearing problems.

**Deafness** A deaf child may not learn to speak at all as he will not be able to mimic sounds, let alone understand them.

Early screening of hearing, starting at six months, is vital, for without it deafness can easily pass unrecognized. Screening tests are carried out at infant welfare clinics and advice on speech-training will be given if necessary.

▼ Speech can be stimulated by reading stories and discussing pictures in books.

# Ailments from six months to five years

The childhood ailments described here are either common ones or among those which tend to cause anxiety in parents.

**Ear infections** Relatively common in pre-school children, ear infections usually affect the middle ear, which is the cavity behind the ear-drum. The middle ear is connected to the throat by a small channel called the Eustachian tube. Germs can pass up this channel and infect the middle ear. Infection is aggravated by the adenoids, which may obstruct the outlet in the throat. The symptoms of ear infection include fever and signs of pain such as persistent crying. Babies will also be reluctant to feed. Ear infections can *only* be diagnosed by passing an inspection instrument gently into the ear-hole so that the inflamed ear-drum can be seen. Antibiotics are always necessary, even though the cause may well be a virus rather than a bacterium, and the most effective antibiotics are those of the penicillin group. If the child's adenoids are substantially enlarged, he may suffer frequent attacks of middle ear infection. Adenoidectomy, or removal of the adenoids, is the usual treatment. Repeated attacks of ear infection may cause the development of a thick, sticky but clear fluid behind the ear-drum. This complication is known as a 'glue ear' and causes hearing loss. The treatment, usually combined with adenoid removal, consists of placing plastic tubes called grommets into the ear-drum to allow drainage of the fluid into the ear-hole, after which the hearing slowly returns to normal.

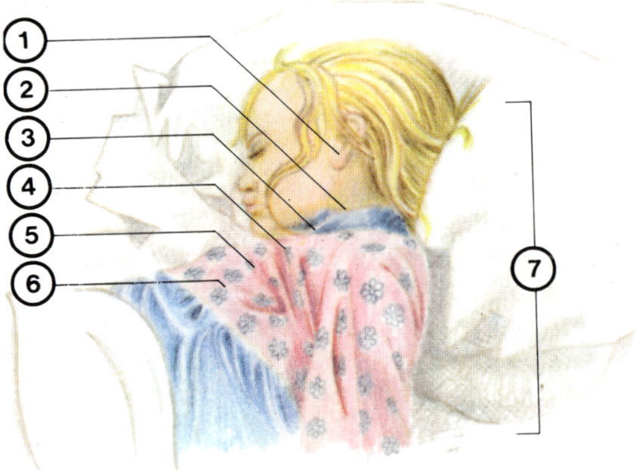


▲ Some of the illnesses to which young children are prone include: **1** ear infections, **2** recurrent sore throats, **3** epiglottitis, **4** croup, **5** bronchitis, **6** asthma, **7** febrile convulsions.

**Recurrent sore throats** Sore throats tend to affect children frequently when they are first exposed to groups of other children, for example, in play-groups and nursery schools. Most sore throats are caused by viruses; bacterial infection is also fairly common. The condition may not necessarily be an infection of the tonsils but of the back of the throat in general. Removal of the tonsils is scarcely ever necessary and is never done before the age of five. The tonsils are responsible for dealing with germs in the mouth and unless abscesses form within the tonsils repeatedly, which very rarely happens, removal of them makes no sense. Paediatricians disapprove of tonsillectomy while ear, nose and throat surgeons, not surprisingly, approve!

Throat infections become less common with age, but tonsillectomy by no means provides immunity to throat infections.

**Bronchitis** This is an infection of the bronchial tubes which can be caused by bacteria or viruses. A runny nose, fever, a cough and a general sense of being unwell constitute the main symptoms. The infected secretions from the bronchial tubes are often coughed up and swallowed and are therefore rarely seen. In infants, who have small bronchial tubes, the secretions cause considerable narrowing, and air is trapped in the air spaces of the lungs. When the infant exhales, a high-pitched wheezing sound can be heard as air is forced out of the lungs through the narrowed tubes.

Bronchitis is not serious in under-fives, being quite different from the chronic bronchitis suffered by the middle-aged. It need not necessarily be treated with antibiotics and seldom lasts long. This condition is known as wheezy bronchitis.

**Croup** Almost always caused by a virus, croup causes inflammation and swelling of the lining of the larynx and windpipe. In young children with small air passages, any such obstruction makes it more difficult to draw air into the lungs. The crowing sound associated with the child's attempts to inhale is known as croup. This sound may be alarming and will become louder when the child cries. It is best to see the family doctor at this point. In most instances, the condition sounds worse than it actually is, but in severe attacks the child's attempts to breathe may become convulsive.

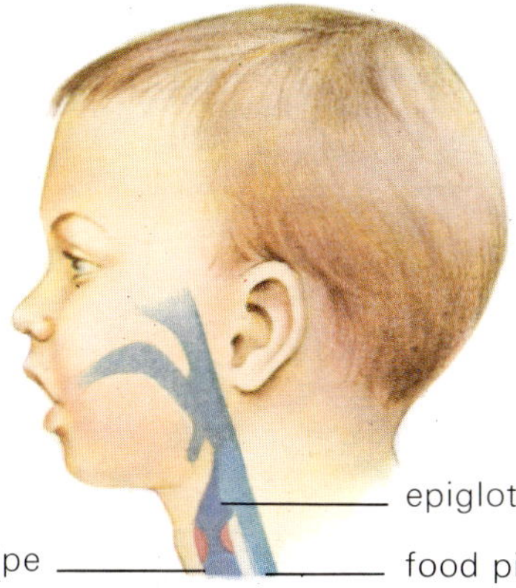


**Epiglottitis** This is an inflammation of the little flap (epiglottis) which guards the entrance to the windpipe. Epiglottitis occurs suddenly and produces the same convulsive breathing pattern as severe croup. Medical advice should be sought at once. The condition is very uncommon but may be fatal unless treated in hospital. No child who has noisy breathing or makes crouping sounds will be suffering from epiglottitis if he is breathing in a relaxed manner.

**Asthma** This ailment causes unnecessary concern amongst parents. Asthma is one of the causes of wheezing, but unlike wheezy bronchitis it tends to be recurrent and continues beyond infancy. Like any symptom, wheezing can be mild or severe. In most children the wheezing is mild. The main problem with asthma is the difficulty in sufficiently emptying the lungs of air when exhaling. The smaller bronchial tubes go into spasm and prevent some of the air from leaving the lungs, which gives the child a rather barrel-chested appearance during the attack.

The spasm of the bronchial tubes is caused by the inhaling of small particles to which the child is allergic. The number of substances to which asthmatics may be allergic is enormous. The individual child is usually allergic only to a few, and one of these will always be the house-dust mite or its droppings. The mite is too small to be seen and is found in almost all houses. It feeds on skin scales and dandruff. It is not

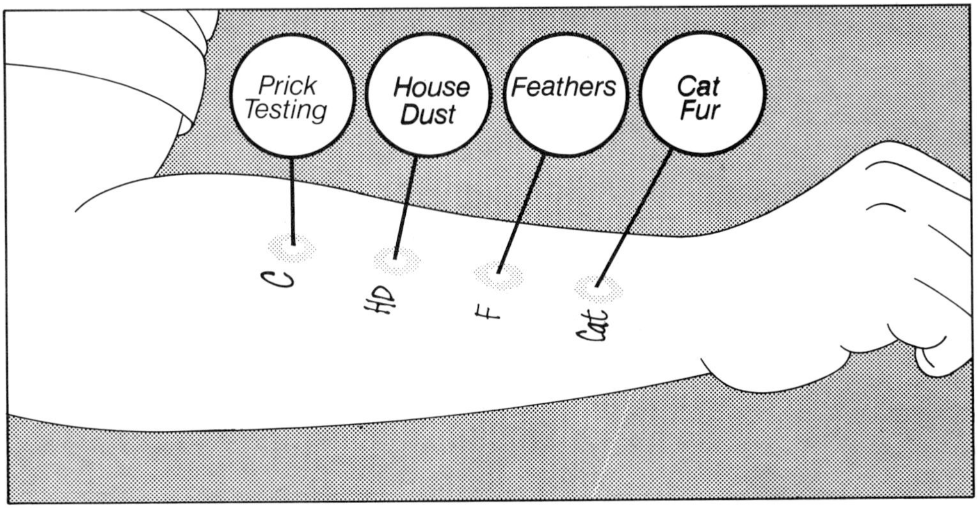


surprising, therefore, that it is commonly found in bedding and dusty environments. Inhalation of house-dust-mite products in quantity will lead to wheezing.

The mite cannot be eliminated from the house but can be kept to manageable numbers by precautions such as washing the blankets and curtains frequently, using polythene coverings for the mattress and vacuuming the bedroom daily several hours before the child goes to bed.

The allergic child will often wheeze after exercise, especially running. Swimming is less likely to cause wheezing. Many asthmatics suffer from, or have suffered from, eczema or hay fever, which like asthma are allergic conditions. Allergy to foods is an unusual cause of wheezing.

A typical asthma attack is heralded by coughing and followed by wheezing. As the mite predominates in the bedroom the coughing and wheezing are most frequent at night or in the early morning. It is frequently the case that the cough is more obvious than the wheeze and unfortunately many children receive antibiotics for their symptoms rather than anti-spasmodics to relax the bronchial tubes.

Wheezing becomes a real problem when it is present most of the time, even though mild, or when there is considerable breathing difficulty. Correct drug therapy is needed, otherwise chest deformity may result and growth may be impaired. Severe difficulty with breathing can be dangerous and requires special medical measures,

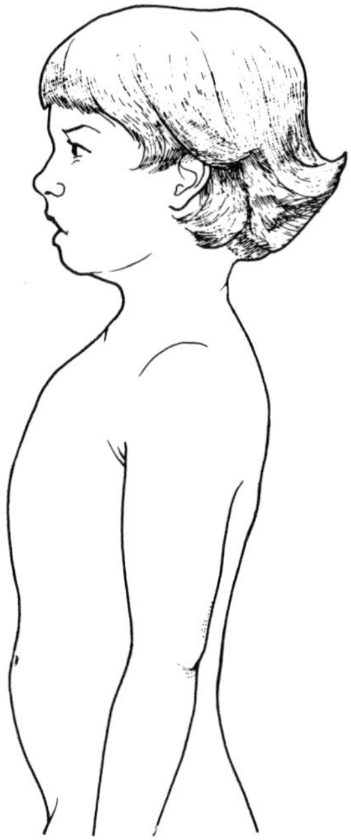

▶ Chronic asthma that has not been adequately treated may produce a mild degree of chest deformity known as barrel chest.

◀ Allergens can be detected by introducing small quantities of the suspected substance into the skin (prick testing). A control substance (usually saline) is also introduced into the skin for comparison. Allergy is proved if the substance in question produces a large lump with reddening of the surrounding skin.

usually in hospital. In the prevention of the wheezing that results when the child inhales substances to which he is allergic, an important advance has been made recently. This is an inhaler which incorporates the drug Intal. The inhaler does not help when the child is already wheezy but is most effective when used four times a day in a preventive capacity. Desensitization to known allergens, or causes of allergic reaction, is helpful in those occasional cases where the child derives no benefit from other types of treatment. Desensitization is produced by a course of injections in which minute doses of the allergen are injected into the skin in steadily increasing doses. The reasons why desensitization is effective where other treatment fails are not known.

**Febrile convulsions** These used to be known as 'teething convulsions' but are nothing to do with cutting teeth. They are short-lived fits accompanied by high fevers and they occur in about two per cent of children. Typically the child will be feverish and suffering from a sore throat, cold or ear infection. He will suddenly become stiff, his eyes will roll up and within a few seconds his limbs will shake uncontrollably. This shaking may last for a minute or two. The child will have temporarily lost consciousness, and will be disorientated on waking up. No special measures need by taken, for by the time the parent realizes what is happening the fit is usually over. There is no cause for panic, but a doctor should be called because at this age there are other causes of fits which, although rare, can be serious. Children who are still convulsing after ten minutes should be taken immediately to a doctor or hospital.

If febrile convulsions occur again during a later illness and the child seems all right after the fit, it should not be necessary to call a doctor.

The best simple preventive measure, to be taken when the child's skin feels hot to the touch, is to sponge the child with warm water and expose his body when his temperature is high. The warm water, being cooler than the child's body temperature, will quickly cool him down.

The tendency to these convulsions often runs in families but the pattern is not consistent. Unlike epileptic fits, febrile convulsions do not occur after the age of six. It is however important to treat the illness which caused the high temperature in the first place. Febrile convulsions affect only children suffering from a high fever, and occur in a very small number of cases.

**Worms** The most usual worm infestation is by thread-worms. These are very common, affecting twenty per cent of children. The only symptom experienced may be itching around the anus. The worms live in the large intestine, usually emerging at night to lay eggs around the anus. The worms look like small threads of cotton and can be seen moving in a recently passed stool. The infection is spread by the swallowing of the eggs, which are carried on the hands of children. Treatment is simple: a single dose of a drug which kills the worms and is often combined with a mild laxative. It is often prudent for the whole family to be de-wormed simultaneously in this way to avoid re-infection.

Treatment for tapeworms is also simple: a special drug is used to overcome the problem.

# Infectious diseases

The well-known infections of childhood that often occur in epidemic form include measles, mumps, German measles, chickenpox and whooping cough. Immunization will protect children from diphtheria and poliomyelitis, which were also once common in epidemic form. Most of these children's illnesses occur only in a mild form nowadays, and are rarely serious. But they can be quite distressing for the child and annoying for the mother if she has other children who have never contracted the disease.

It is not necessary to keep a child with an infectious disease confined to bed, unless he feels too unwell to be up. Attempts to do so are in practice rarely successful! Nor is there any need to worry about the child passing on the disease to his brothers and sisters. These conditions tend to be at their most infectious during the incubation period when the disease has not yet shown itself, so the disease will generally be contracted from a child who is not yet known to be suffering from it. Similarly, if the infected child is going to pass on the disease to his brothers and sisters, he will probably have done so before his own symptoms have developed. New babies under six months are in many cases protected from common infectious diseases by the antibodies which have been passed to them in the womb. However, the mother cannot pass on antibodies to her unborn child unless she has suffered from the disease herself at some time, nor can she pass on immunity to whooping cough.

**Measles** Measles can be a distressing condition, sometimes with unpleasant complications including ear infections, pneumonia and, rarely, an infection of the brain called encephalitis. Measles can be prevented by immunization, preferably carried out when the child is just over one year of age. As most cases of measles occur after this age, immunization is strongly recommended.

The disease is caused by a virus and in common with all virus infections it does not respond to antibiotics. The virus is spread by minute droplets from the nose and throat of an infected person. The first signs of the disease appear around ten days after exposure to a sufferer and include cough, fever, a runny nose and red, runny eyes. The rash appears three or four days later as blotchy spots, which usually begin behind the ears and around the hair at the nape of the neck. This spreads to cover the

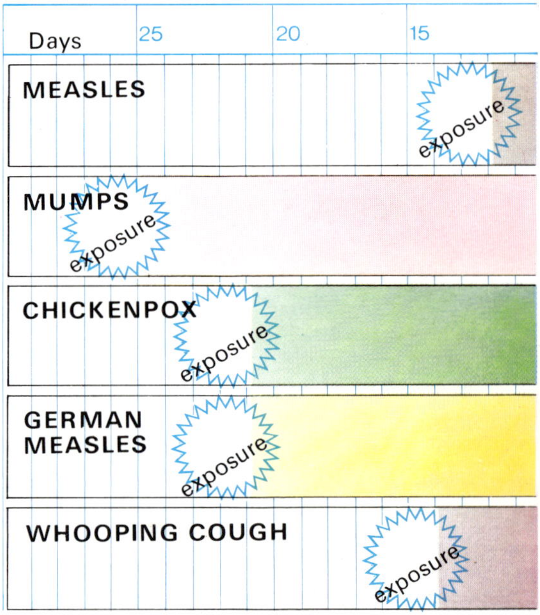

whole skin surface over the next two days and disappears altogether within ten days of its first appearance. The course of the disease is usually mild, but otitis media (middle-ear infection) and pneumonia, caused not by the virus but by the bacteria which replace it, occasionally follow. These infections will need antibiotic treatment.

Occasionally, as a result of the fever from which he is suffering, an infected child may have a fit shortly before the rash appears. The fit will be very short-lived and there is no need to panic for the child will soon recover fully.

No special nursing measures are needed for measles apart from general comforting and seeing the child has enough to drink. The child with measles is capable of infecting others for seven days after the rash appears, so he should not go into public places until this period has elapsed. Then he can go wherever necessary, including school, providing he is well.

**Mumps** This disease is also caused by a virus and is spread by droplets from the nose and throat. In the under-fives it is usually mild and not nearly as infectious as measles. The virus affects the parotid (salivary) glands which are located in the cheeks close to the angle of the jaw. These glands become swollen and painful, producing an obvious facial swelling. One or both glands may be affected and the child will have some discomfort when chewing. The incubation period is long (three weeks) and there are not usually any symptoms before the facial swelling has begun. The child's temperature will usually but not invariably be higher than normal at this time. The swelling and pain will last from

▼ The incubation period for each infectious disease is shown on the left (indicating the maximum period in which the disease can be expected to develop after contact with an infected person). To the right is shown the maximum time from first symptoms to complete recovery.

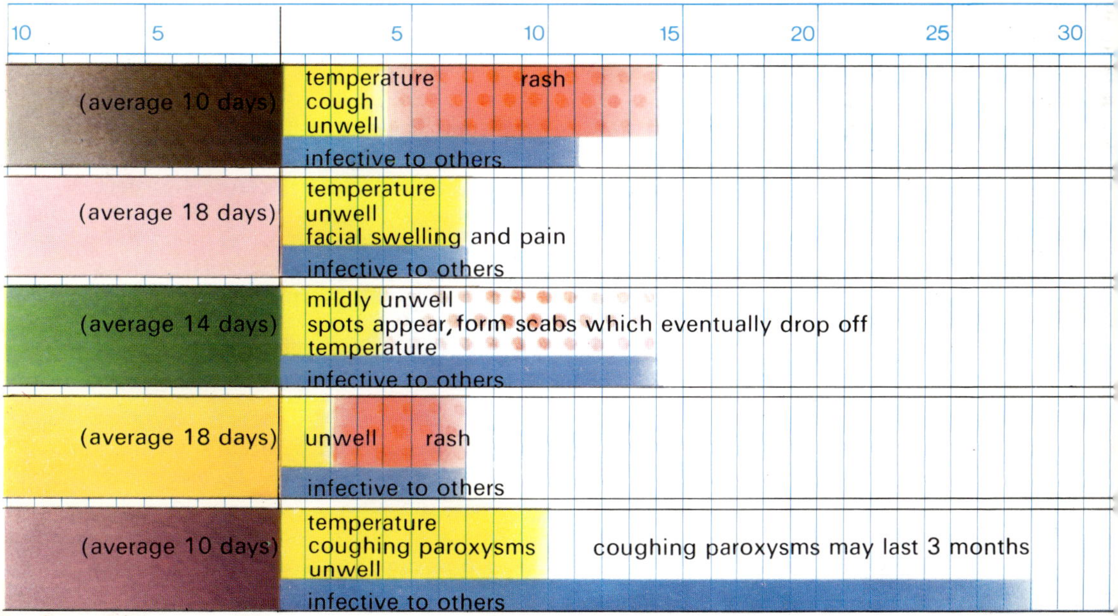

three to seven days and the child will be infective until these symptoms have disappeared.

Complications are infrequent and very rarely serious. About one in four hundred sufferers from mumps develop meningitis which occurs at any time up to ten days after the facial swelling. Headache and a sore neck are the usual complaints and complete recovery, without treatment, is to be expected. In very rare cases, permanent deafness in one ear can result from mumps. Infection of the testicles, another complication, does not occur before puberty.

A mumps vaccine is available but is not in general use because this is not a serious disease and the cost of vaccinating entire populations would be far greater than that incurred by the disease itself.

**Chickenpox** This is a viral disease which is extremely infectious. It is extremely mild, with an incubation period of up to three weeks. The spots appear on the trunk and are raised, resembling tiny blisters. They spread to the limbs and face over the succeeding four days and tend to be quite itchy. The tops fall off the small blisters and leave small depressions behind—pockmarks. If these are scratched and become infected they may leave small unsightly scars. For this reason, it is best to avoid scratching, particularly the face. The condition is infective until the blisters have scabbed and dropped off. Complications are extremely rare.

**German measles** The disease is caused by a virus which like mumps is spread by droplet infection. It is an exceedingly mild disease characterized by a pink rash which begins on the head and spreads to cover the whole skin surface within thirty-six hours. The rash is not itchy and lasts for three days. The infected child will be mildly unwell for a day before the rash appears and have a mildly elevated temperature. The incubation period is two to three weeks after exposure. The disease can be infectious for up to ten days after the rash has appeared. Though very mild, it causes severe malformations in the unborn child if the mother catches it during the first three months of pregnancy. It is for this reason that the child sufferer should be kept indoors until no longer infective. Complications in pre-school children are remarkable rare.

A german measles vaccine is available and should be offered to all girls at puberty, so that they will not bear malformed children. A blood test can be done to check whether any girl or woman has had the disease.

**Whooping cough** This is a severe disease in children under six months. Unfortunately whooping cough immunization is not effective in this age group and will not prevent the disease occurring. However, the greater the number of immunized individuals in the population, the less common the disease will be and the smaller the risk of catching it. Over the age of three, the condition is mild and causes little harm as a rule. The incubation period is a week, at the end of which the child develops a running nose and cough. The cough occurs in great bursts making it difficult for him to catch his breath. When he does so he sucks air into his lungs with a loud crowing noise, or 'whoop'. He will often vomit after such a paroxysm. The child will be infective for a month. The cough may persist for many months after the lungs have returned to normal, but that is all it is—a cough. If it keeps the child awake at night it may be necessary to give a cough suppressant. Nowadays complications are uncommon, but in previous generations whooping cough was a cause of prolonged lung disease.

# Hygiene and feeding techniques

**Feeding with artificial milk necessitates very high standards of hygiene for all the equipment used. Until the baby is old enough to start dairy milk feeding from a cup, all his feeding equipment should be sterilized. When he is about four months, weaning can begin, and a sensible eating pattern established for all his childhood years.**

### Sterilizing bottles and teats

The milk, the bottle and the teat must all be germ-free to prevent the risk of gastro-enteritis. After nine months, the baby will have built up his own resistance and thereafter sterilization of his food containers will be unnecessary.

It is best to set aside a special work surface for preparing feeds, close to running water and facilities for boiling. Plastic laminate surfaces are ideal, being easily cleaned and free of germ-harbouring cracks. Bottles and teats can be sterilized either by boiling or by soaking in a special chemical solution for 3-4 hours.

Boiling, which takes only 15 minutes, is far quicker. Clean the bottle and teat carefully first. To clean the bottle, use washing-up liquid and a special wire-handled brush. Rinse the bottle inside and out with tap water before boiling. Clean the teat as shown, under a running tap. It is easier to do this preliminary cleaning immediately after the bottle has been used. Then immerse both bottle and teat in a saucepan of water.

The disadvantages of the boiling method is that for ideal sterility only one bottle should be sterilized at a time. It is not desirable to boil several bottles in a large saucepan because after an hour or so the water in which the bottles are immersed will no longer be sterile.

The chemical method allows a large number of bottles to be sterilized at one time. The most commonly used solution is sodium hypochlorite (trade name Milton). It is sold in a concentrated form and requires dilution. A special container for the solution and bottles can be purchased. However, a plastic bucket is just as good, providing it is used only for bottle sterilization and is cleaned out regularly. It is helpful to number the bottles with a marking pen to ensure each one remains in the solution for at least 3 hours. The bottles do not require rinsing after removal from the container, though some parents like to rinse out the insides with boiling water.

Of these two methods, most mothers find soaking the most practical and time-saving.

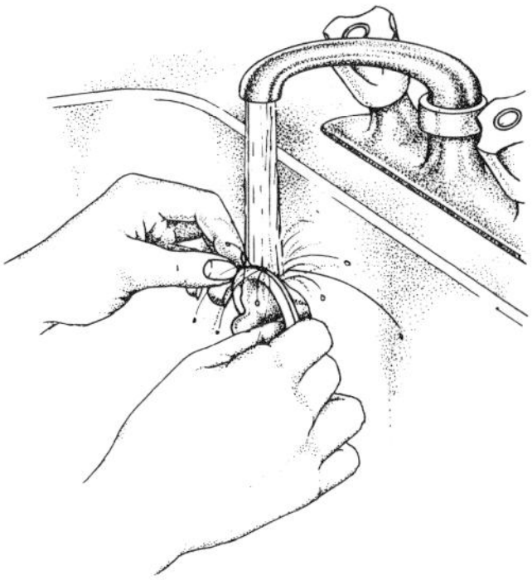

▲ Remove milk particles with a brush. Invert the teat and rub with the fingers under a tap.

## Teat holes

The size of the teat hole is important: too large an opening will cause choking and spluttering; too small a hole will require considerable effort to suck from and cause unnecessary swallowing of air (and therefore excess wind). The hole can be enlarged by pushing a red-hot paper clip through it, making sure to hold the other end in a pair of pliers. Old teats may perish and become soft, collapsing when sucked and thus yielding no milk.

## Preparation of milk for bottle-feeding

Either a liquid milk concentrate or dried (powdered) milk can be used. Liquid preparations can be poured directly into the bottle and then diluted, according to the instructions on the container, with boiled water.

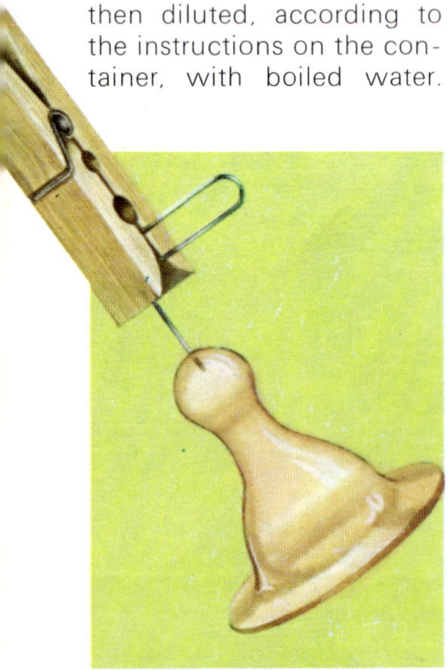

▲ Hold the red-hot paper clip with a clothes-peg when enlarging the teat hole.

The container should be kept in the refrigerator once opened. Dried milks can be mixed in the bottle as a rule, but some need to be mixed in a sterile jug (made of heat-resistant glass) before being poured into the bottle. The scoops provided should first be filled with the powder then levelled off with a sterilized knife blade.

## Milk temperature

Many mothers like to warm the feeding bottle in hot water, or in a special bottle-warmer, before using it. (If this is done, test the temperature by pouring some milk on to the back of the hand.) However, there is no good reason for warming the bottle; indeed, most hospitals use only cold feeds.

## Winding

Whether breast- or bottle-fed, all babies swallow air when feeding and will need encouragement to expel it – 'winding'. There are two basic methods. One is to sit the young infant on the knee with one hand supporting the chest and the other gently tapping the back. The other is to hold the infant over your shoulder and gently tap his back. The essential principle is to hold the child upright, in order to allow the air bubble in the stomach to rise to the right position for expulsion.

Wind is blamed, usually mistakenly, for a variety of discomforts. Unnecessary air swallowing should be avoided by attention to the teat hole.

▲ When bottle-feeding, support the head well in the crook of the arm.

## Weaning

'Weaning' means gradually replacing a total milk diet with solids. There are no special rules: the process is one of trial and error. Weaning should begin when milk alone does not satisfy the child, a stage usually arrived at when he is about four months of age, or slightly earlier with some infants. It should not be left later than nine months, because after that age it will become progressively more difficult. Unless introduced to solids and spoon-feeding in good time, the infant may react by spitting out his food; he will also need vitamins to supplement his milk diet.

In commercially-produced baby foods, carbohydrate tends to be the first choice of solid for weaning, usually in the form of baby cereals or rusks, but there is no reason why meat or vegetable should not be given. Obviously, ordinary solid food should be puréed to begin with to make it easy for the child to swallow and adjust to the different texture. Many types of puréed foods are available in cans or jars. It is worth tasting these commercial baby foods, for their palatability varies a good deal. Purées can be prepared at home with a liquidizer too, of course. Mothers who do this will not only know for certain what their baby's meal contains, but will save money. As commercial purées often taste different from the foods from which they are derived, the use of homemade purées can also make the transition to normal food a smoother process for the baby.

Introduce one flavour at a time and do not persist with anything to which the infant seems to take an instant dislike. Start with one semi-solid feed a day, gradually increasing to three a day over the next two months. At about eight months the food can become coarser, to encourage a chewing action and accustom him to food pieces rather than thick liquids. Although an eight-month-old child will not yet have the right teeth for chewing, he will be able to cope in much the same way as a toothless old person. By one year, most children will be eating a finely chopped-up version of an adult diet.

Right from the start, it is as well to provide a balance of protein (meat, egg, etc.), carbohydrate (rice), and vegetables. However, young children rarely like strong-flavoured foods such as cheese before the age of one year and often not until much later.

### Eating habits

Once a child begins to prefer feeding himself, he may develop strong ideas as to what he will and will not eat. Never try to force-feed a child with food which is 'good for him'. Force-feeding produces an acute aversion to food in general.

If the child refuses to eat anything but biscuits, stop providing biscuits, offer an alternative, but do not attempt to make him eat it. No young child will starve himself to the extent of losing weight, so his health will not suffer. Although he may not eat the alternative food at first, hunger will eventually prevail upon him to do so!

Some children pick at their food at meal-times and leave the table at every opportunity. Those who apparently do not eat are usually filling themselves with sweets, biscuits and soft drinks between meals. Between-meals snacks should be cut out and, whether he is eating or not, the child should be made to remain at the table until everyone else has finished.

▼ Do not fuss if the child makes a mess in his early attempts at using a spoon.

# Cuddling and play

**The physical comforts of cuddling and play are vital to a child's emotional and mental development. Cuddling provides security, comfort and basic animal warmth, while play is a child's means of exploring his environment, giving him the opportunity to experience and experiment with everyday life. As the child gets older, he will encounter more formal games, which introduce to him the discipline of rules and the concept of give and take.**

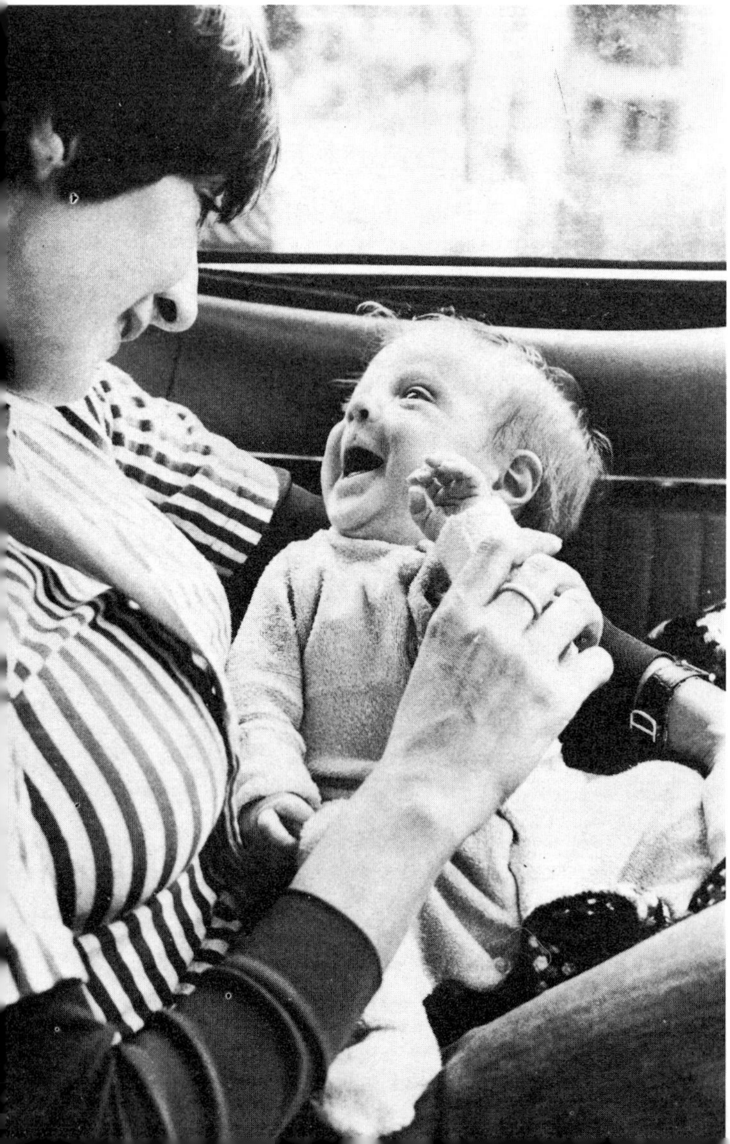

The warm bodily contact of cuddling is an extremely important element in the early formation of a good child-parent relationship. The human infant responds to the warmth of his mother's body, gentle rocking and softly spoken words. Breast-feeding, of course, can provide all these sensations; bottle-feeding provides close contact, but the child is not necessarily in contact with the mother's skin.

Infants always recognize the unique way in which their own mother handles them, and during the early weeks they may react to any unfamiliar touch, however gentle, by becoming restless and even crying.

As the child gets older, he will probably become less sensitive. He will start to enjoy more boisterous cuddling, with a lot of kissing and laughter.

The need for close physical contact continues for much longer than is generally realized. Many ten-year-

◀ Cuddling and talking to your baby will give you a pleasurably relaxed feeling. Eye-to-eye contact is of great importance.

olds, for example, still like to get into bed with their parents first thing in the morning. For pre-school children, cuddling is especially welcome when they are tired and irritable.

No child who obviously needs the comfort of cuddling should be rejected because the mother is tired or busy.

Some children need much more cuddling than others. This trait is a reflection of the child's feeling of uncertainty towards the outside world. If his needs are met at an early stage he will develop confidence in due course. It is impossible to overdo cuddling if this is what the child wants, but at the same time it is advisable to seek the causes of his lack of confidence. If he is completely protected from all the minor difficulties of everyday life, he will never develop self-confidence and will eventually be very confused.

**Physical play**

From one year onwards, children's play becomes increasingly physical. Usually, the young child will begin by enjoying the sensations of being tickled, lifted on to the shoulders and bounced on the knee by his parents. When he can walk, he will delight in chasing games. However, some children are less enthusiastic about boisterous play and may even be frightened by it. In such cases, the child should not be subjected to activities he does not enjoy.

One activity which many fathers revel in is throwing a young child into the air and catching him – a very dangerous practice; in children under two years, it could cause brain damage, because the sudden acceleration and subsequent deceleration of the young brain within the skull may instigate bleeding on the surface of the brain.

Another early type of play is based on the popular 'baby bouncer', a sort of suspended harness in which the child bounces up and down by pushing himself off the ground with his feet. Many infants of nine to twelve months or so enjoy this, but it is a repetitive activity which stimulates neither physical development nor social behaviour.

▲ Some babies enjoy being in a baby bouncer, hung from a lintel. The child is completely safe and well supported by the webbing.

Another popular contraption is the baby walker, a broad-based frame on wheels in which a child can stand with his legs through the holes of its canvas inlay. So positioned, a child who is not yet walking can propel himself around a room. However, using a baby walker does not hasten normal walking and may in fact delay it.

Some parents are keen on taking very young infants

swimming, a practice which is harmless enough provided the child is not frightened in any way by the experience. Although it is possible to teach even one-year-olds to swim, this will not make them future champion swimmers. The achievement will serve mainly to gratify the parents' egos.

Older children revel in physical play – a fact which is usually obvious from three years onwards, when chasing games, racing and wrestling will be highly popular. By this time they will be playing with other children as well as with their parents.

### Physical aggression in play

It is difficult for a three-year-old to control his aggression at times and possibly even more difficult for him to understand the aggression of others. Angry physical exchanges will usually be short-lived: a blow or kick will be followed by a rapid withdrawal. Prolonged physical aggression is abnormal and should be checked quickly by taking the aggressive child away from the others. Gentle recrimination and a watchful eye on the part of the parent are essential. At the same time, it pays to be objective about children's fights and not let them cause trouble between you and the parents of your child's playmates.

Television violence may be reflected in children's play but always as a re-enactment of action the children recognize as sham.

### Imaginative play

All children indulge in games of imagination. Often they will choose common objects or toys as concrete extensions of their fantasies. For example, small boys will use toy cars to push into the furniture, meanwhile providing sound effects, while girls will earnestly admonish their dolls for bad behaviour.

The private world of the child's imagination cannot be entered by the parent, though the theme of play may sometimes be obvious: hospital games and 'mothers and fathers' will be familiar to most parents, and may indeed provide insight into the children's inner anxieties or aggressions.

Aggression during fantasy play is not abnormal, though it may reflect conflicts in the child's emotions.

Parents should never interfere in fantasy play. If, during such play, a boy decides to enact a female role or vice versa, there

▼ The physical interaction of boisterous play between brothers and sisters is part of growing up.

▲ Guns are less symbols of violence than interesting objects for toddlers.

► Games of hand-clapping—like 'pat-a-cake'—can be learnt at a young age.

would be no point in a parent trying to impose a more conventional sex role. Nor should parents try to ensure that girls play with dolls while boys confine themselves to more 'masculine' toys.

A common occurrence in childhood is the invention of an imaginary friend, with whom the child will have conversations and share his activities. He will probably expect his friend's likes and dislikes to be recognized and accommodated by his parents in addition to his own. Such inventions are quite normal, and not surprisingly more common among 'only' children. The invisible friend, probably with well-defined characteristics, is an aspect of the child's inner personality.

**Organized play**

When the child is about four and is beginning to grasp the concepts of rules and fair play, he will start to appreciate organized games. The rules must be simple at first, and cheating cheerfully tolerated! Simple dice or card games of a repetitive nature are a good introduction. More complicated games can be introduced when the simple ones cease to amuse.

Four- and five-year-olds greatly enjoy ball games, the rules of which are generally too complicated to capture the interest of the very young. By all means allow the child to invent his own games, even though his rules may be completely incomprehensible to you as a parent.

**Verbal play**

This type of play begins at about four months of age, when the infant starts joyfully experimenting with noise. By fifteen months or so he will be able to play games with his mother based on simple rhymes or repetitive expressions. By two and a half years he will enjoy nursery rhymes, for both the words themselves and the rhythm of their delivery. At three years, with a larger vocabulary, certain words will amuse him, and he will repeat them endlessly to anyone who will listen. He will enjoy games in which objects have to be named and make involved 'conversation'. These verbal games serve to increase the child's vocabulary and ability to express himself.

# Social behaviour

**Some form of discipline is essential for all young children, for unless they are given a framework in which to operate, they will not be able to judge the effect of their actions upon others. To provide this disciplinary framework, parents will need to be both tolerant and consistent in their own behaviour.**

Punishment can never be effective unless the wrongdoer understands what he has done wrong. Without understanding on the part of the child, punishment is merely revenge. The two-year-old who realizes that if he tries to lift a pot of tea he will be smacked will appreciate the concept of cause and effect but not that his action may endanger him.

Children under one year never consciously act in a way which is designed to anger a parent, so punishment has no point at that age. Although he may realize that certain behaviour excites pleasure in his parents, he will be slower to appreciate displeasure. Loving tolerance – although it will come under stress at times – is the best attitude for children of this age.

It is not really possible to 'spoil' a child of less than a year. Spoiling indicates an uncritical, permissive attitude which allows a child to indulge his whims at an age when he *does* have some concept of what is and is not reasonable behaviour – from about eighteen months.

Most spoiling tends to be inconsistent, with excessive tolerance on some occasions alternating with irritation and smacks on others.

▲ Occasional outright defiance is normal. It is an attempt to establish the boundaries of acceptable behaviour.

Smacking is not an easy way of obtaining good behaviour, though it may serve to relieve a parent's feelings on occasions. Children over three may be given a sharp smack for repeated wrongdoings provided they know what they have done wrong and why it was wrong. However, it is important to keep smacking to a minimum and not to use it as an indiscriminate expression of annoyance. Smack the child in hot blood, immediately, and ensure that the reason is obvious to him. *Never* smack a child under one year old.

Parents are frequently influenced by the experiences of their own upbringing, for better or worse, when disciplining their own children. Rather surprisingly, parents who had a strict upbringing themselves tend to treat their own children strictly. Lax parents should be aware that their indulgence may not only ensure trouble for them in later years, but ingratitude from their child, whose life could be blighted by an indulgent, and perhaps non-caring, upbringing.

## Parental self-control

The need to chastise a child under one year, or to cause severe injury to any young child when meting out 'punishment', is abnormal. Parents who find themselves likely to succumb to such feelings should seek expert advice immediately. Many mothers who injure their children are psychiatrically depressed after the birth without realizing it. The condition is very common, and to seek help from a doctor or health visitor is the first step to overcoming it. Early treatment can almost always prevent a calamity.

# Pot-training and night control

**Older generations set great store by early bladder- and bowel-control, though they knew little of its normal speed of development. For this reason, mothers who are pot-training children should try to ignore comments from outsiders, especially older in-laws, on the subject. Normal progress, as outlined below, varies from child to child.**

Normally a child will be ready for some form of pot-training by the age of two. Before fifteen months, he will be incapable of understanding what the pot is for, and any occasional successes before this time will be happy accidents rather than conscious efforts to use the pot. Similarly, the child's consciousness of a desire to pass urine or empty his bowels will not be evident before one year of age. Neither will his ability to 'hold back'.

At about fifteen months, some children show recognizable signs of being about to defecate—perhaps clutching their bottoms or merely ceasing play and looking thoughtful. It may be worth placing the child on a pot on such occasions for a few minutes, without insisting that he remain there. If the child does pass a stool, by all means show pleasure, but do not show annoyance if he decides not to remain on the pot.

These early attempts serve mainly to introduce to the child the concept that a pot is for receiving urine and stools. Never hold an unwilling child on a pot: this will almost always delay success and may cause tantrums. On the other hand, unless the child has been shown what the pot is for, he cannot be expected to demand removal of his nappy.

Most children can be pot-trained by between eighteen and thirty months, but some take until three years. Normal children are always clean and dry in daytime by four years.

Some children obstinately refuse to use a pot, although they may not object to sitting on one. It is often helpful in such cases to remove the child's nappy for part of the day. Having previously been in nappies all the time, the child will be used to voiding into them, and he will find the new sensation unpleasant. Although at first he may continue to wet and soil, he will soon find the pot a desirable alternative.

Night control is usually achieved about six months after day control. There is little that can be done to accelerate this naturally acquired skill, the timing of which varies from one child to another. About one in ten children still wet the bed occasionally at five years, but this is no cause for concern. Restriction of fluids, punishment and parental emotion do not help. Patient handling with suitable praise for dry nights, is the best approach. Bed-wetting, after all, is merely a nuisance — not a disease. It frequently recurs following some emotional shock, such as the arrival of a new brother or sister, a death in the family or simply starting school.

▼ The main features to look for when choosing a pot are stability, a wide rim (for comfort) and a bowl that is not so large that the child sits *in* it rather than on it.

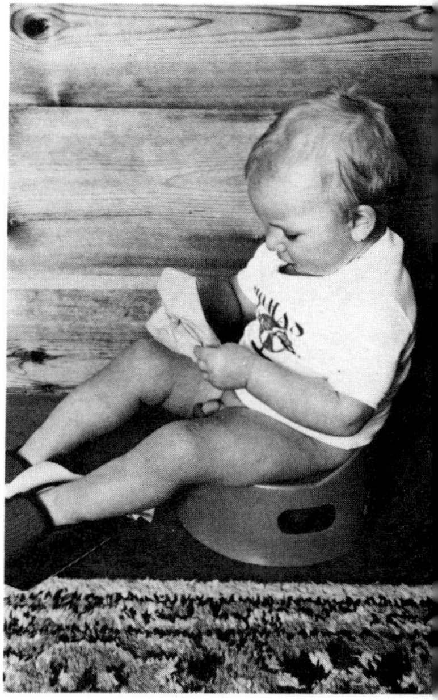

# Dental care

**Proper care of the primary teeth will prevent many unpleasant visits to the dentist in the child's later years. Parents can help by cutting out unnecessary sugary foods and between-meal sweets from the child's diet and by providing fluoride toothpaste to strengthen tooth enamel.**

Once teething has stopped, dental care for the young child is essentially prevention of decay, or caries. To prevent decay is both easier and cheaper – for the individual as well as the state – than treating it.

The surface of the teeth is covered with a hard layer of enamel which forms a barrier against the germs which cause decay. Weak enamel provides access to germs which attach themselves to the teeth in association with saliva and particles of food to form plaque. Sugary substances in food combine with the germs in the plaque and form acids which attack the enamel. The main aims in preventing decay are to strengthen the enamel to make it more resistant to attack by these acids; preventing plaque formation by careful brushing and cleaning; avoiding sticky, sugary foods whenever possible; and using dental floss to prevent plaque formation along the line of the gums, which can cause chronic infection. The latter is the main cause of loss of teeth in adult life.

Strengthening of the enamel can be achieved by an adequate intake of fluoride. This element occurs naturally in water, but its concentration varies from country to country and from region to region. Those in areas with a normal fluoride content in the water have much less dental decay than those in, for example, the many urban areas in which the water contains very little

◀ From about the age of fifteen months, a child's teeth need regular brushing. At the beginning, it can be regarded as a sort of game. The average child will need to be supervised when brushing his teeth until he is five and can manage satisfactorily on his own. The toothbrush should have a small head to allow each tooth to be cleaned individually, a flat surface and soft bristles. The inner and outer surfaces of each tooth should be brushed from gum to tip. Worn brushes should be speedily replaced. Electric toothbrushes are more effective than ordinary ones and fun for older children, though they may frighten younger ones.

▶ The worst devices for encouraging decay are comforters such as Dinky Feeders filled with sweet drinks. The child tends to keep the comforter in his mouth, bathing the teeth in sugar almost continuously. Most children who use these filled with sweet drinks need all their teeth extracting by the age of five, as these teeth were. ▼

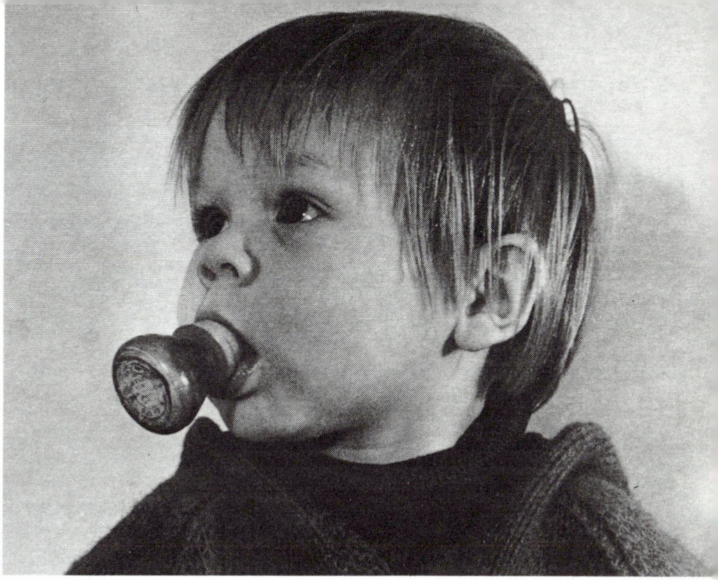

fluoride. Where the local water is low on fluoride, dentists strongly advise that fluoride tablets be given daily to children up to sixteen. The tablets are very small, contain 1 mg of fluorine, are tasteless and can be dissolved in any drink. Children under two years need half a tablet daily and those over two one tablet daily.

Regular brushing of the teeth after each meal is highly recommended, though not always possible; failing that, teeth should be brushed at least twice daily, morning and evening. If teeth-cleaning is not possible after the midday meal, encourage the child to fill his mouth with water, swirl it about and then spit it out.

Many commercial drinks advertised as containing plenty of Vitamin C also contain large amounts of sugar flavoured with rosehip or blackcurrant. Never give these to a child. Sweets are harmful too but will do less harm if eaten just before a meal. Sugary chewing gum and toffees are very harmful indeed. The best tactic is to prevent the child developing a sweet tooth: do not give him sweet foods, least of all as a reward for achievement or good behaviour.

Dental floss is a form of thread which is inserted between the teeth to remove food and plaque that toothbrushes will not remove. Pre-school children do not have to use dental floss because they have big gaps between their teeth in which food is less likely to lodge permanently.

Dental check-ups should begin at three years. They serve two important functions: to accustom the child to the dentist (as it is unlikely that the child will need any treatment on his first visit, no unpleasant procedures will be necessary and the child's memories of the visit will therefore be pleasant); secondly, advice and instruction on dental care will be given, and, of course, if there *are* signs of decay, the dentist can deal with them.

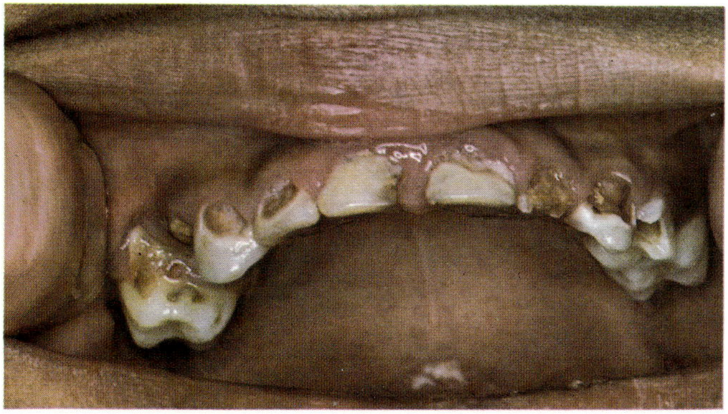

# Child-care facilities

**Day nurseries are intended for the supervision of infants and young children. The earliest age at which children are accepted is six months but in special circumstances they may start earlier. Play-groups accept any child under five, but he will usually have to be over a year to benefit. Nursery schools accept children from two and a half to five years.**

For the many families in which, for economic or other reasons, both parents must work, and for one-parent families, day nurseries can often solve the problem of where to leave a pre-school child during the working day. Though some establishments may provide little else, all will at least give the child the benefit and stimulation of socializing with children of his own age. Play-groups and nursery schools provide rather more: the groups of children are generally smaller than they are in day nurseries, and the staff are therefore able, in most cases, to devote more time to organizing stimulating activities for the children rather than merely keeping order.

## Day nurseries

All local authorities finance a number of day nurseries, whose staff are specially trained to look after pre-school children. The number of such nurseries varies considerably from area to area and, unfortunately, is rarely related to local requirements. Even in those areas where there are private as well as local-authority nurseries, the demand always exceeds the supply. Parents are expected, where possible, to make a financial contribution, which helps towards the cost of providing the children with midday meals. This payment is waived in cases of severe hardship, as in the case, for instance, of a single mother receiving social security payments.

In poorer areas, many of the places at local-authority day nurseries are reserved for deprived children. The recommendations for places are usually made by community child-health doctors at the request of health visitors or social workers.

Otherwise, day nurseries provide a reasonable alternative for all mothers who cannot look after their children themselves during the working day, or during part of it. Children will undoubtedly benefit from the contact with other children and with a sympathetic staff, and social relationships will be stimulated. In the case of children whose speech seems slow in developing, this is of great value.

In general, however, a day nursery is a poor alternative to a good child-minder because within the large groups typical of most day nurseries it is not possible for staff to give children individual attention. Pre-school children need one-to-one relationships wherever possible.

## Pre-school play-groups

These informal gatherings of pre-school children are organized by interested volunteers who have some experience of looking after young children in small groups. Some of the organisers have had special training in child care but most have not.

Usually the organizers take pains to provide their charges with constructive play activities in a free-and-easy atmosphere. Water-play, painting, group games, singing and listening to music are among the chief activities and the expertise of the organizers will vary, so any parents contemplating a play-group for their child would be well advised to visit several before making a choice.

A timid child will find large, noisy groups intimidating, while a self-assertive child will usually settle in quickly. Similarly, play-groups which are too highly organized will not suit those children who (like many adults) need periods when they can simply dream, relax and do nothing. This is a need which parents often

▲ Mothers are encouraged to stay and help out at play-groups, where the atmosphere is always free and easy. The sessions are usually for a morning or an afternoon.

fail to recognize, and which constant enforced socializing in a play-group may prohibit. Therefore, the final choice of play-group should be influenced by the personality of the child in question.

Play-groups normally function during the mornings only, but children may spend from one to five mornings a week there. At most play-groups a small charge is made for attendance, but some are free. Parents are always welcome to stay and help at play-groups if they wish.

**Nursery schools**

These, run by qualified teachers, are for children over three, and are intended to provide a preparation for the formal schooling which will normally begin at five years. Nursery schools accustom the child to being a member of a group and to participating in group activities. Not all children take kindly to such involvement initially, but most nursery-school staff will ensure that the process of integration can be a gradual one if necessary.

The range of activities varies from one nursery school to the next. Formal education, such as reading and basic numeracy, is not usual, nor perhaps desirable. The aims of the nursery schools are to familiarize each child with everyday group activities, explain the world about him, answer his questions and build up his confidence.

Much of this simple everyday education is achieved by play and group games. It is usual to find many different activities going on simultaneously. Ideally, these will be tailored to the diverse needs and interests of the individual child.

Children who have attended a nursery school will find the transition to formal school less difficult than children accustomed only to the home environment.

At present, there is a great shortage of state nursery schools. Most are therefore private, and charge a modest fee. The small fee is a worthwhile investment, even for the less well off. Unfortunately, it is the child who lacks stimulation in his home environment who would most benefit from attending nursery school – and whose parents are less likely than most to be willing to pay the charges, however modest.

In the private sector, as with play-groups, nursery-school attendance can be varied. A combination of mornings and afternoons is usually possible. State nursery schools require whole-day attendance, however, and are therefore ideal for mothers in full-time employment who have children of nursery-school age.

# Preparation for school

**Starting school can be very frightening for some children. The reasons for some of these fears may be obvious, while others may be difficult to guess. Prior awareness of the stresses that the child is likely to experience on starting school will help parents to cope when the child gives his anxieties emotional expression—which he will probably do at home.**

On arrival at school, the child will be projected into a large group of children for longer than ever before. The full force of their number will be felt most forcibly during play breaks, when perhaps several hundred children will be tearing about with their established friends. This situation will bewilder, even frighten, many children, especially those who are timid or unused to large gatherings of children. A child who has spent most of his time at home will also find it far harder to adjust to being away from his mother for a whole day at school, and this could undermine his confidence for a while. By far the best way to prepare a child for the experience of school is to accustom him to similar situations in the form of nursery school or play-groups, or by taking him to visit parks and playgrounds during the year before he starts school. Some primary schools run parallel nursery classes, which provide the child with an ideal means of transition to 'big' school.

It is a very good idea for parents to inspect the prospective school's toilet facilities. Many are smelly and unpleasant and many lack privacy, having no locks on the lavatory doors, for which reasons many children will never defecate in a school toilet, but will hold back (not always successfully) until they reach home. Children will seldom explain the reason for such 'accidents'. (This is perhaps the sole good reason for encouraging defecation on rising.)

Most schools have basic rules regarding dress and will issue leaflets advising parents what to buy. It pays to observe children who already attend the prospective school before spending money on special clothing. Otherwise, you may find yourself buying uniform items that are only ever worn by new arrivals! Few schools insist on complete uniformity of dress among their five-year-old pupils. Individual items of

Even if there are few doubts that the child will be able to settle happily into primary school, it is advisable to show him the school well in advance. Most head teachers like to meet their prospective pupils before they start and may even offer to show them round too. Other parents whose children attend the school will be able to tell you whether it has any particular procedures about which the child should be warned.

School will almost certainly affect the child's behaviour at the end of the day. Expect uncharacteristic irritability and aggressiveness and try to remain calm while soothing the child's ill temper. The cause will be partly over-reaction to the organized regime of school, partly exhaustion. However free and easy the school, it is inevitable that structured activities will dominate the school day – far more so than at home or even at nursery school. Quiet moments for day-dreaming will be far fewer: hence the over-reaction on returning home. The end-of-day exhaustion is typical of most five-year-olds, however active, on starting school. In time, the child will become used to school routine, and will feel less tired on his return and therefore less irritable.

Emotional preparation can be as important for the mother as for the child. It is often a greater wrench than she would ever have expected to leave him at school on the first day. It seems to mark the end of an era, the end of the timeless days at home. Every mother is bound to miss her child at first. If he is her only child, she would be well advised to plan some social activities to fill this first, lonely day rather than being alone at home.

clothing should be selected with a view to easy dressing and undressing. Many children find multiple buttons difficult to deal with in a hurry and zips are a better alternative. Similarly, the child will appreciate easy-to-fasten shoes, such as ankle boots with zips. If he has lace-up shoes, make sure that he can tie them himself and that the laces are not so long that they require multiple double bows.

School lunches could also cause problems, not simply because the food is likely to be unfamiliar to the child, but because consumption of it may be preceded by a great deal of pushing and shoving. For the first term, it may be best to arrange for the child to have school meals only two days a week, preferably at the beginning and the end of the week, because the experience of a full day's absence from his mother may take a little while for him to accept happily. After a term, review the situation and increase the number of lunches – i.e. full days at school – if there seems to be no problem. The lively talk and socialization that occurs during school meals, in a context of neither strict discipline nor total lack of control, can play an invaluable role in building up a child's confidence. The food itself will vary from school to school. Contrary to popular belief, many children do enjoy school meals.

# Learning through leisure

**It may seem surprising to use the term 'leisure' in connection with pre-school children. Their entire active existence, it might seem, could be classified as leisure. However, this is not really the case. Any activity in which the child does not wish to participate, such as a shopping trip, will not be leisure for him. Of the many leisure activities children enjoy, the following are usually popular.**

While older children may have specific hobbies and take part in organized sports, leisure for the very young child is simply spare time in which the child, and probably one of his parents, participate in a mutually enjoyable activity.

At a very young age, such activity will consist of the mother talking to the child and encouraging his speech. If this takes the form of a game in which simple rhymes are related to him, his enjoyment of the sounds and rhythm will be obvious from his interest and laughter.

### Stories

A child of two years will enjoy simple stories, but they must be short to hold his attention. Three-year-olds like hearing the same story over and over again and are often able to memorise the whole tale. Parents can prove this to themselves by deliberately changing one or two sentences of a familiar story and observing the child's instant and indignant reaction to the change.

As the child becomes older, he will enjoy different types of story, and may well prefer the more dramatic tales. Pre-school children often seem to have an almost morbid interest in violent tales and killing. This is not because they are naturally cruel by temperament but because they have no experience of them. Children will quickly appreciate that adults are uneasy about the subjects of violence and death and will accordingly become very curious. Their interest in these topics will be stimulated more by their taboo nature than a childish delight in gore itself.

Some children find certain fairy tales frightening because the retribution suffered by the 'bad' characters will seem to be at variance with their own experience of life. Wicked characters, especially those with magical powers, will have no real everyday equivalent with whom the child can compare them, and he may fear that he could one day encounter someone like that. Fairy tales with evil characters that could prey on the child's consciousness are best avoided as bedtime stories, which should ideally provide a pleasant, warm and relaxing end to the day.

### Painting

Most young children, especially from the age of three onwards, will find painting an enjoyable pastime. All children make a mess when painting, so it is wise to take suitable precautions to avoid damage to carpets and furniture so that the child can paint without constant warnings to be careful. His initial efforts will be crude, but he should be allowed to experiment with a good deal of paper and a minimum of parental direction. Colours, rather than forms, will be his main interest at first.

### Water play

Another leisure pursuit which younger children love is water play. If there is a garden and warm weather, a small paddling pool will be a source of endless pleasure. The child will enjoy emptying it with small buckets and putting gravel or soil into it.

### Ball games

At four to five years ball games, especially football, will become popular. These games help to accustom children to the concept of rules and fair play. Ball and racket games are not very suitable for pre-school children as their co-ordination will not yet be good enough to cope efficiently with the equipment and they will be frustrated by their lack of success.

**Card games**
Simple card games become interesting to children at between four and five years. Standard playing cards have the advantage of encouraging the child to recognize numbers and to check, if necessary, by counting the pips displayed. Simple board games using dice will also encourage counting skills. It is remarkable how quickly a young child will learn to identify the number of dots displayed on the dice.

**Television**
It is almost inevitable that watching television will quickly become a favourite leisure-time pursuit of the majority of children. Provided the television is not allowed to become an electronic baby-sitter, that parents are available to watch with the child or at least to answer his questions, and that programmes are selected with the child's age in mind, television can make a real contribution to the child's education. Pre-school children will not listen to a commentary for more than a minute at a time. They will prefer to watch and ask questions of their parents. No educational function is achieved, therefore, by placing a child in front of a television set and leaving him to watch it alone, however interesting the programme may be.

Prolonged, indiscriminate television viewing seems to produce a remarkable passivity in some children. The visual content is more attractive to children than the audible matter and prolonged viewing may in fact delay the child's development of linguistic skills. Television can in fact make the child a poor listener.

As regards specific content of television programmes, it is important to realize that certain programmes can frighten some children. Knowledge of your own child's particular fears should to some extent dictate your selection of programmes for him to watch. Generally, it is reality as opposed to fantasy which frightens most: violence in news programmes will scare children because they will recognize it as real, whereas ritualized violence of an unreal nature, as in cowboy films or cartoon shows, will do no harm because children know instinctively that they are stories rather than fact.

◀ Children's first attempts in the creative arts are likely to be messy but enjoyable.

# Toys and pets

**Toys are an integral part of the normal development of children. They provide a valuable key to the understanding of the world at large and wide scope for the child's imagination.**

To a child, a toy is any object which pleases him. Quite often, what parents regard as a fascinating toy will be dismantled by the child, who will then derive endless pleasure from its components. Parents must expect and accept such situations!

It is wise never to buy a toy solely for its potential educational value. The child is likely to show a disappointing lack of interest in the toy. After all, there can be few people, whatever their age, who like to be given 'improving' presents regardless of their likes and dislikes.

The type of toy children tend to like most is the cheap, 'rubbishy' sort rather than the pricier, better made and well-finished article preferred by their parents. However, cheap metal toys with sharp edges, small plastic toys which can be swallowed and cheap soft toys with eyes attached by metal spikes should be strictly avoided.

It is important not to buy expensive, mechanical toys which perform one or two repetitive and unalterable functions: these toys will rapidly bore the average child. A good toy is one that can be put to a variety of uses and can be incorporated in the imaginative aspects of play.

On the whole, young children prefer to have a variety of inexpensive toys rather than a single expensive toy, but will become more specific in their demands as they grow older.

No toys should be considered to be suitable for only one sex. As a matter of principle, attempts to confine boys to suitably 'masculine' toys and girls to 'feminine' ones are both misguided and unnecessary. Similarly, it is unwise to supply a child *only* with toys that, like bricks or paints, have no gender at all. A variety of toys should be provided so that the child can select those he wishes to play with: he will usually play with them all.

## Toys for infants up to one year

Babies of about four months delight in mobiles and in a line of rattles strung across their pram or cot: interesting shapes and colours fascinate them.

By five to six months, the child will be grasping objects and trying to take them into his mouth. The type of object does not matter much, providing that it is not impregnated with toxic substances or likely to splinter easily. It should also, ideally, be narrow enough for a small hand to grasp and light enough for the child to manipulate easily. Spoons, small rattles, plastic rods and cups are suitable.

Soft toys are more endearing to parents than to babies of this age. When the baby is about nine months old, however, soft toys will come into their own, being ideal for him to throw out of his cot or pram without causing any damage.

Many one-year-olds like playing with paper, especially tearing it up and scattering the pieces.

They will also enjoy pushing a ball around on the floor. For the very young, a large, multi-coloured ball is more exciting, because it will be less easy than a small one to lose: balls small enough to hold in the hand are easily lost under armchairs and cupboards, and at this age 'out of sight' means 'out of mind'.

### Toys for children from one to two years

Many children begin to walk at between twelve and fourteen months. As the child's normal position becomes more constantly upright, he will enjoy pushing a toy wagon with a suitably high handle. He will derive even more pleasure from the wagon if he has something to load into it, such as some bricks which are small enough for his hands to grasp (that is, with sides of about 2·5 cm or 1 in).

Young children also like small model cars, containers in which small objects can be placed and objects which can be struck noisily.

At eighteen months or so, children can cope with containers which accept only certain shapes, but the shape-matching should not be too complicated or frustration will result.

### Toys for children from two to three years

By now the child will be ready for crayons. He will enjoy scribbling with different colours and will probably use up a good deal of paper. Rolls of lining paper are economical for this purpose.

At two and a half years, the child should be ready to cope with a paintbrush and poster paints. If he is to paint indoors, it is advisable to lay a ground-sheet down in the middle of the room for him, well away from the walls, where he can be as messy as he likes.

At this age, children like to imitate their parents doing the housework, using small dust-pans and brushes and toy carpet sweepers.

Toy garages for toy cars and dolls' houses with miniature furniture are much appreciated at this age and will provide plenty of scope for imaginative play. They allow the child to observe the workings of the outside world while controlling it in his mind without interference.

### Toys for children from three to five years

As the child's horizons expand, so will his capacity to use different types of toy effectively. Small plastic construction bricks which fix on to each other are ideal. Given a pair of small, round-ended scissors, the child will enjoy cutting pictures out of magazines and will revel in the sticky messes he can achieve with these and a supply of paper paste.

At three and a half years he will be able to manage a tricycle or small pedal car, having mastered by now the alternating action of the legs needed to propel them.

At four to five years, he will be able to assemble simple tracks for toy cars alone and will be completely absorbed by the activity.

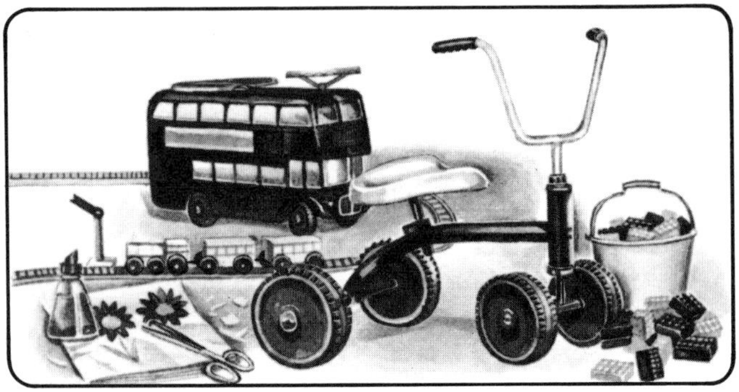

Simple card and dice games will amuse him now that he is developing an appreciation of rules and their application. Some five-year-olds can even manage a game of draughts.

### Children and pets

Pre-school children are not capable of caring for any pet properly by themselves. It is best for any pet acquired to belong to the family as a whole, the parents or older children undertaking the feeding, watering and cleaning. It is important for the parents themselves to like the chosen pet and be concerned for its welfare. Under no circumstances should an animal be given to a young child as if it were merely an addition to his collection of toys.

### Tricycles and bicycles

From three-and-a-half years the tricycle will provide much pleasure. Tricycles designed for younger children will usually be propelled by pedals which are attached directly to the front wheel, without a chain. These can in fact be more difficult to ride than the conventional type driven by a chain which turns the back wheels. The latter are faster and easier to control but it is difficult to find one small enough for the average three-year-old. Most modern bicycles for the very young are fitted with stabilizers, which are two small wheels attached to the rear hub by two strong metal supports. Stabilizers make the balancing technique easy. Soon the child will no longer need to rely upon them.

# Safety in the home

**Accidents in the home cause more injuries to the pre-school child than any other type, but most can easily be prevented by a little forethought. Pre-school children should never be allowed near a public highway without supervision and should therefore never be in a position to be knocked down by a motor vehicle.**

▲ Keep all dangerous substances well out of children's reach, including medicines, which should be locked up.

Fatal accidents in the home are suffered by about 500 pre-school children a year. The majority are babies that die of suffocation or choking. Many of these deaths occur when babies are prop-fed – that is, left to feed themselves from a bottle propped in position in their mouths. Suffocation often occurs when young children put polythene bags over their heads.

The rate of non-fatal but serious injuries is also high. One investigation has shown that 35 per cent of all home accidents occur in pre-school children, although they represent only 10 per cent of the population. The highest incidence occurs, not surprisingly, amongst the more mobile and adventurous two-to three-year-olds.

## Burns and scalds

These tend to happen to children who are inadequately supervised, most frequently in homes where no commonsense measures have been taken to prevent such accidents.

A typical scald occurs when a child reaches out to grab a tea-pot or tea-cup, probably situated above his head, and is sprayed with extremely hot fluid. Scalds can cause considerable disfigurement and often require plastic surgery. It makes sense, therefore, to keep all containers of hot liquids well away from the edge of tables or cookers. Never lift a teapot over a child or leave an unattended saucepan on the cooker.

Also common among children are burned hands caused by touching an unguarded or inadequately guarded electric fire. All fires need efficient guards that cannot be pulled over by toddlers. Avoid using unstable free-standing paraffin heaters where there are toddlers.

## Head and limb injuries

Young babies often suffer head injuries when they are having their nappies changed: left momentarily on a table while mother searches for a safety-pin, it is easy for a baby to roll off on to the floor. For this reason it is important to make sure everything is to hand before bathing or dressing an infant. If you are interrupted – for instance, by telephone or door bell – pick the baby up and take him with you rather than leaving him unattended.

Two-year-olds often hurt their heads by walking into corners of tables. Eye injuries can also be caused in this way. Although it is not easy to ensure a completely safe environment for an adventurous toddler, there may be some measures parents can take if they consider their home through the eyes of their child, who is probably less than a third of their height and considerably more unsteady on his feet! If your living accommodation is cramped, for example, sharp-cornered furniture should be removed where possible.

Children of four and over love climbing up to open windows. A fall from the first floor can kill or cause irreversible brain damage. Never assume that an open window is inaccessible to a young child. Unsightly though they may be, temporary wooden bars across possibly dangerous windows can save lives. Bolts can be used to prevent sash windows being opened more than a few inches.

A common cause of limb injury is the spin-dryer, which can sever a child's arm if opened while in operation. Never leave a toddler unattended in a room with moving electrical equipment.

Sharp implements of all kinds and breakables that become sharp implements on breakage should be kept well out of reach. Staircases should be gated to stop toddlers using them without supervision and thus risking accident.

**Poisoning**

In the UK, about 50 children a year die of poisoning, while the incidence of non-fatal poisoning is very common indeed. If there is a toddler about, keep cleaning fluids, paint stripper, turpentine and paraffin out of reach in eye-level cupboards, *not* under the sink.

Accidental swallowing of medications, especially aspirins, tranquillizers and sleeping pills (all of which are potentially lethal), is also common. If a child should take any medicine not intended for him, stick a finger down his throat to induce vomiting, then take him to the emergency department of the local hospital, with a sample of the substance if you are not sure of its identity. *Never* give salt in water to produce vomiting. If absorbed, the salt could cause brain damage.

▼ A special child-gate at the top or bottom of a flight of stairs will prevent adventurous toddlers falling down them.

# Immunization table for under fives

| Age | Vaccine | Interval between doses | Remarks |
|---|---|---|---|
| 0–12 months | Diphtheria, tetanus, whooping cough and oral polio (first dose) | | Can be given at 3 months but better immunity is achieved if given at 4–6 months. |
| | Diphtheria, tetanus, whooping cough and oral polio (second dose) | 6–8 weeks | Diphtheria, tetanus and whooping cough are given all together in one injection (the 'triple'). Not to be given if the child has a raised temperature, nor if he is having steroid drugs. |
| | Diphtheria, tetanus, whooping cough and oral polio (third dose) | 4–6 months | Omit whooping cough vaccine if child or his relatives have had fits. |
| 1–2 years | Measles | single dose | Usually given at 18 months. Not to be given within one month of polio vaccine or other live vaccines, nor if the child has had fits, is allergic to eggs, or has close relatives with epilepsy. |
| 5 years | Diphtheria, tetanus and oral polio (booster) | single dose | Can be given at 3 years. |

The above chart shows when immunizations should be carried out to protect young children from disease.

# Height and weight tables

There are great variations in the normal height and weight of children. The height of a child is obviously related to the height of the parents, in particular the so-called 'mid-parent height', which is the average of the sum of the heights of both parents. In Britain the average mid-parent height is 168 cm (5 ft 6 in). The speed of longitudinal growth (height) is most rapid during the first two years of life and steadily declines until puberty when there is a sharp increase.

Although tall children tend to be heavier than children who are short or of average height, there are many exceptions. A child who is increasing in height at the normal rate but is very thin is nonetheless healthy. Disease or ill-health which slows down the child's weight gain will also slow down the normal gain in height. Excessive weight gain is unhealthy. Fat infants tend to become fat children and later fat adults. The death rate is considerably higher among fat adults. The foundations for a long life are effectively laid in childhood.

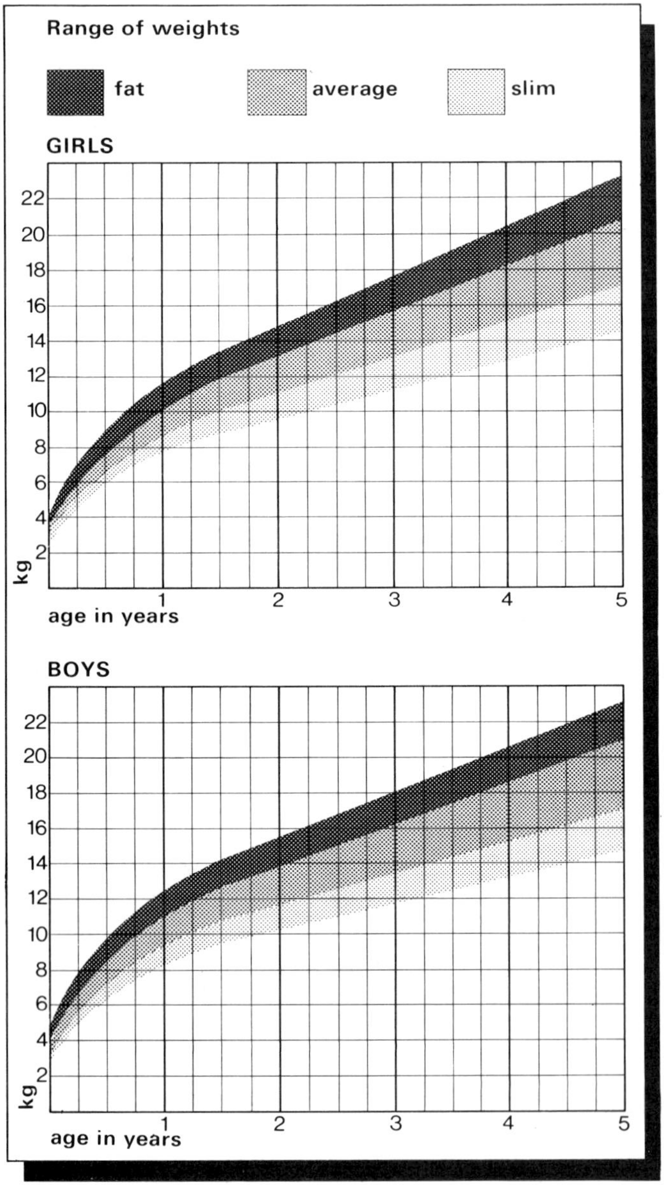


**Weight ranges in childhood**
The ranges shown in the tables (from slim to fat) include 95 per cent of the population. Children who exceed the weight given for their age in the 'fat' area are obese unless they are tall or very tall. Those who weigh less for their age than

indicated in the 'slim' areas are mostly normal but some may be abnormal, especially if their height gain is abnormally low.

**Normal heights in childhood**
The tables shown here start at two years, because children below that age, with the normal forward curvature of the spine typical of infancy, are unable to stand up straight enough to be measured accurately. The tables have five categories: very tall, tall, average, small and very small. Ninety-five per cent of the population will range from the small to the tall category. The very small category is normal if the mid-parent height is small or very small, but abnormal if the parental height is average. Very few diseases produce excessive height and all are extremely rare.

To measure a child's height accurately requires special equipment. Parents can obtain a good approximation if they do it in the following way. The child stands with his back against a wall, while one parent makes sure his knees are straight and his heels are on the ground and the other parent places one hand under his chin, pulling his neck gently upwards. With the other hand, a large book is placed on the top of the child's head at right angles to the wall. A mark is made on the wall corresponding to the lower edge of the book and the distance to the ground is measured with a tape measure.

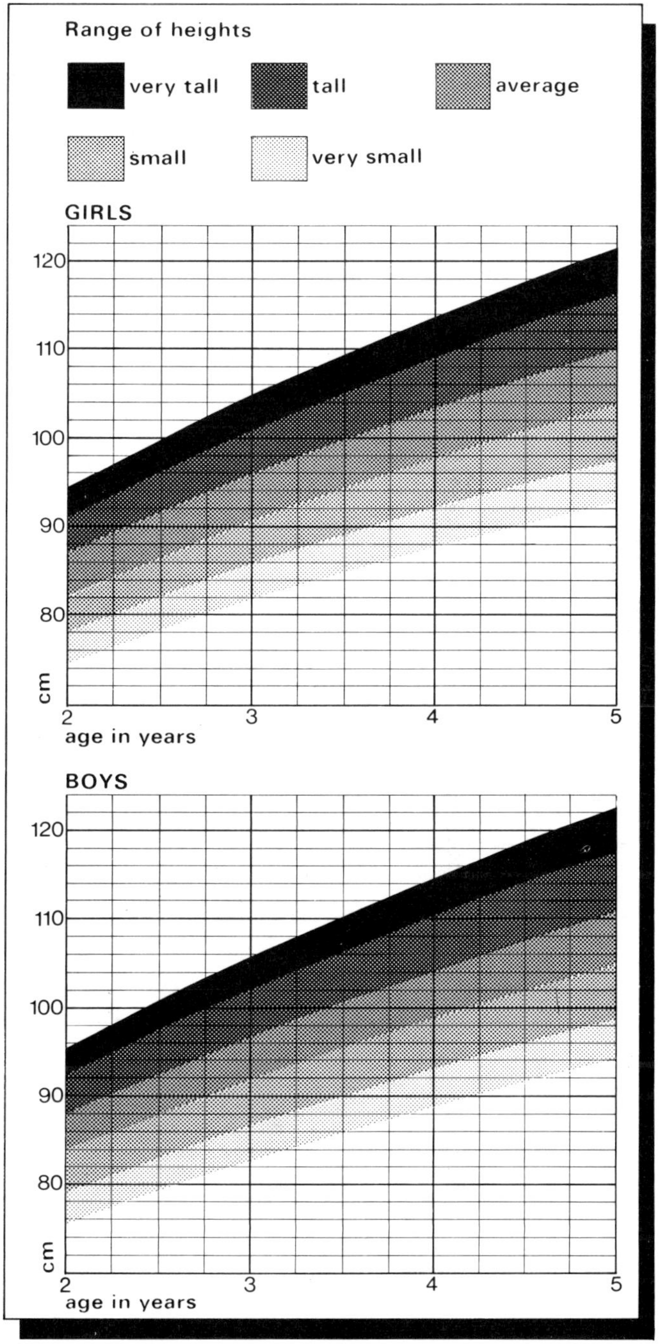

# Social security benefits

This section deals with social security benefits relating to children, as outlined by various leaflets issued by that government department. As these leaflets contain more information than can be included in this short section, their salient features will be summarized. The actual rates of cash benefits given are those quoted in leaflet NI 196 of the Department of Health and Social Security issued in November 1977. For each category of benefit mentioned below a leaflet number will be quoted. For full details, therefore, the relevant leaflet should be obtained from a social security office or post office. All rates quoted are correct at the time of going to press.

**Assessing entitlement to benefits**
A useful pamphlet, M 11, issued by the Department of Health and Social Security, shows how to work out what entitlements are available. This simple, straightforward document provides a convenient check-list for assessing the family's total income, including state benefits of various kinds, if already being received, and, in another section, all its weekly needs. Outgoings of all kinds, including mortgage and life insurance payments and repayments, are individually itemized. Once the income and the needs have been separately totalled, the form can be sent to the local social security office, where the entitlements of the family in question will be worked out. Many of the benefits available to parents of pre-school children are described in the pamphlet.

**Child benefit**
(leaflet CH 1)
Introduced on 4 April 1977 to replace the old family allowances, this takes the form of a cash benefit of £2·30 per week for each child (whether natural or adopted) and for one-parent families an extra £1 a week. Application for this benefit, which is available to all, should be made on form CH 2, obtainable from social security offices. Birth or adoption certificates must also be submitted. An order book will be sent to your local post office; this contains a number of orders which can be exchanged for cash. These may not be cashed in advance but may be allowed to accumulate for up to six months. The benefit ceases for each individual child at 16 years, or at 19 years if the child is receiving full-time education or undergoing an apprenticeship. There is no means test or exclusion on the grounds of high parental income. The benefits are subject to income tax, if the parents are liable for it. Full details are given in the back of the child benefit order book.

**Family income supplement**
(leaflet FIS 1)
This can be claimed by parents if, despite one of them working full time (30 hours or more per week), their total family income is less than £43·80 per week. Child benefit does not count as part of the total family income. The supplement to which the family is entitled is the difference between the total family income and £43·80.

**Attendance allowance**
(leaflet NI 205)
This is a tax-free allowance for people who are severely disabled physically or mentally and require considerable attention from a third party. In the case of a child this will normally be one of his parents. There are two rates of benefit: the higher rate is for those who require constant attention by day and night; the lower rate is for those who need this by day only.

The qualifying requirements are as follows: by day, continual supervision to avoid danger to the disabled person or others and frequent attention by day with regard to bodily functions; by night, similar criteria apply. For children under 16 years the attention required must be substantially in excess of that normally required by a child of the same age and sex.

The amounts paid in attendance allowance are £14 for the higher rate, £9·30 for the lower rate.

*Children under two years are not eligible for the allowance.*

**Child's special allowance**
(leaflet NI 93)
This is a special payment made

to divorced women in the event of the death of a former husband who was, until he died, supporting their child, or children. This allowance can be paid in addition to the normal child benefit. However, if other national insurance benefit is already being paid in relation to the child or children, only the higher of the two benefits will be paid. For the first or only child, the allowance is £7·40 per week; for each other child, it is £6·90 per week.

**Guardian's allowance**
(leaflet NI 14)
This is a weekly payment made to those who look after an orphan of under 16 years (19 years if in full-time education), such as relatives or foster-parents. The allowance may also be paid to a divorced parent who has been awarded custody of a child or children and whose former partner is neither maintaining the offspring nor liable under any Court Order to do so. Occasionally the allowance may be awarded to a foster-parent when the child has one parent living but in prison for a prolonged period. The amount paid is, for the first or only child, £7·40; and for each other qualifying child £6·90.

**Free milk and vitamins**
(leaflet W 11)
Milk and vitamins are free for expectant mothers and all children under school age. If a family is receiving supplementary benefit or a family income supplement, they are awarded automatically. Milk and vitamins are also free for all but the first two children in families with more than three children under school age. Applications can be made on form FW 9, available from social security offices.

Milk only is free for all handicapped children aged 5–16 years who are *not* registered pupils at any school, including special schools for the handicapped. Applications can be made on form FW 20, obtainable from social security offices. Children attending an approved day nursery, play-group or child minder's are eligible to receive $\frac{2}{3}$ pint of milk free on days on which they attend.

Those entitled to free milk will receive seven pints per week or two packs of artificial milk powder (for infants). Those entitled to free vitamins will receive two bottles of vitamin drops every thirteen weeks.

If a family's income is below a certain limit, regardless of whether the parent or parents are in full- or part-time employment, all the children below school age (including foster-children) are eligible for free milk. The social security office will advise on eligibility.

**Prescriptions**
These are all free to those under sixteen years of age, regardless of the cost of the drugs or for how long they need to be administered. Occasionally, special diets are prescribed by hospitals that are not technically prescribable by the family doctor on the standard form. If not deemed a recognized drug, the family doctor may find he has to pay for these items himself. Where this difficulty arises, and it is rare, the best course of action is to let the hospital consultant know at once. He will then make arrangements with the hospital pharmacy to order the items. Collection will be necessary, but the cost should be borne by the NHS.

**Glasses**
These are free for pre-school children and this includes the frames also, providing they are the standard National Health Service children's frame. If adult frames are needed for a child under ten years for some reason both the lenses and the frames must be paid for.

**Dentures**
These may seem a rather unusual item for the pre-school child but unfortunately the need is not as rare as it ought to be. No charge is made for dentures for pre-school children.

**Free school meals**
The local education office or Education Welfare officer will advise on eligibility for free school meals, which are available only to families with low incomes.

**Death grant**
(leaflet NI 49)
This is a lump sum paid in the event of the death of a child to help with funeral expenses. The amount paid depends on the age of the child at death. If the child was under 3 years, the amount is £9; aged 3–5 years (inclusive), it is £15.

The foregoing information is intended simply to provide general guidance. Your local social security office will supply further information, including all the leaflets mentioned above and others including those on maternity benefit (leaflet NI 17A), earnings-related supplement (leaflet NI 155A), widows' benefits (leaflet NI 13) and, in the event of the death of a husband at his place of work, industrial death benefit (leaflet NI 10).

# Children, parents and the law

In law, 'children' are defined as those up to the age of 14 years, while a 'young person' is someone between 14 and 17 years.

In criminal law, a child is not considered to be responsible for his actions until he is 10 years of age. Most offenders against the law who are under the age of 17 years are dealt with by the Juvenile Courts. Each court is presided over by three magistrates who are advised on detailed points of law by a Clerk of the Court.

An enormous amount of legislation is passed, and regularly updated, to protect children. A recent example is the Children Act of 1975.

**'Care'**

For various reasons, children are occasionally taken into the care of the local authority. For example, if a child is orphaned or abandoned by his parents or parent, someone must look after him and be legally responsible for him. The Social Services department is legally responsible within each local authority. Children may also be received into care when one or both of their parents is admitted to hospital and there is no relative to look after them. Such a step is never taken without the consent of the parents, except on the rare occasions when it is impossible to obtain the parents' consent. For this reason it is known as 'voluntary care'.

The Social Services are responsible for finding the child a suitable place to live, in either a children's home or a foster home. Both of these will have been registered with the local authority; indeed, many children's homes are financed and run by local authorities. Children can also be removed from the parents against their wishes if necessary, mainly in cases of cruelty towards or neglect of the child by the parents.

When children are not receiving adequate care at home, the Social Services or the police can make application for the case to be brought to the juvenile court, as a result of which the court may make an order removing the child from home. They may also place the child under supervision at home. These cases are known as Care Proceedings and need to be based on good grounds for the court to prove the case.

In court, the Social Services can be represented by a Solicitor who is employed in the legal department of the local authority. The solicitor may engage a barrister if he thinks it necessary. Likewise, the child's parents are entitled to be represented by a solicitor or barrister and, if they qualify, to receive legal aid to pay for these services. During the court hearing, witnesses will be called to give evidence of the alleged offences against the child and will be examined and cross-examined in the usual way. Three magistrates will then decide whether the case for a Care Order is proved and what action to take in the best interest of the child.

In the case of a child considered to be in immediate risk of injury or further injury a Place of Safety Order can be obtained. This might be necessary if a child is admitted to hospital with injuries thought to have been inflicted by the parents. The order is intended to prevent the child's parents from removing him from medical care, or to ensure the child's safety while the appropriate authorities investigate the situation. Obviously the grounds for such an order must seem reasonable.

The Place of Safety Order, which can be obtained from a magistrate on application, serves to place the child under the care and supervision of the Social Services for a period *not exceeding* 28 days. After 28 days, the Social Services must either return the child to his parents or appear in court with an application for a Care Order.

Sometimes enquiries into a case may not be completed, or the parents may not have been able to obtain adequate legal representation or, as happens quite often, the court may not be able to meet within the 28-day period for a long enough time to give the case a fair hearing. In such circumstances, an Interim Care Order can be made to extend the period until a full hearing can be given. Parents have the right of appeal if their child is taken into care. The case will be heard in a Crown Court and decided by a judge.

A child in non-voluntary care cannot be discharged from care by the Social Services without application to the original Juvenile Court or to that in whose area the parents now live. It has become possible in some cases for the court to appoint a person who represents the child's interests (a guardian *ad litem*) to ensure that it is both safe and desirable for the child to leave care. This step is taken *in addition* to the protective procedure which is already part of the magisterial system.

Parents can apply for their child to be discharged from non-voluntary care by application to the Juvenile Court. The shortest interval at which they can do this is three months. Failure to succeed does not mean they cannot apply again on subsequent occasions.

### Adoption

Couples who wish to adopt a child should approach their nearest Department of Social Services. Every local authority is required to provide adoption services in its own area. In addition, the local authority keeps a register of various voluntary adoption societies. However, there is as yet no central register of all these societies. The 1975 Children Act stipulates that a service for the assessment of prospective adoptive parents and counselling for those with related problems must be provided. Although it has not yet been fully implemented, most authorities now have an expert on adoption working in their Social Services department.

Each adoption agency, whether a voluntary society or run by the local authority, has its own criteria for the suitability of adoptive parents. These are not statutory criteria but matters of general policy which are determined by the agency concerned. Many of the agencies are run by religious bodies, and these tend to specify that the prospective adoptive parents are of a specific religious persuasion. General considerations as to suitability include the age of the prospective adoptive parents (thirty-five years is generally the upper limit) and the stability of the marriage.

The 1975 Children Act also stipulates that local authorities must provide facilities, including temporary board and lodging, for mothers who wish to have their child adopted.

Third-party adoption, that is, adoption arranged between individuals rather than through approved societies, is still legal but likely to be prohibited soon. The fact that no one will be allowed to apply for an adoption order unless the child has been under the control of a local authority or of a voluntary society for at least twelve months will discourage third-party adoptions. However, if the child has already been in the care of the prospective parents for twelve months or longer, they may apply for an adoption order.

# Advice centres

The following is a list of some of the many organizations which can provide parents with specific help and/or detailed information in cases of difficulties or needs which relate to their children. Many of the organizations were formed by people who have encountered similar problems and therefore know exactly what sort of help and information is likely to be of use to parents.

### The Social Services

The brief of this organization is extraordinarily wide and covers all age-groups. As far as the family with pre-school children is concerned, there are many ways in which they can provide support in the case of difficulty.

Sometimes the help will be financial, sometimes practical – as, for instance, in guiding parents through the bureaucratic procedures that might otherwise deter them from trying to solve their problems.

Every local authority has a Social Services department. In large towns and cities, there is usually a separate department for each district, so that no one should be out of easy reach of a social services office. Overall control of the social services in each local-authority area is maintained by the Director of Social Services, to whom initial enquiries or notifications of problems should be sent. Each area subdivision is organized by a senior social worker, known as an 'area team leader', who is responsible for the work of a number of subordinate social workers, including those who do the 'case work'. The system is organized so that the area team leader and senior social workers are aware of the problems that the case workers are experiencing and can give them practical advice and moral support.

The case-worker is the person who has the main contact with the department's 'clients'. Contact may be initiated either by a visit from the 'client' to the social worker *or* vice versa. Medical social workers might, for example, visit the parents of a child who has been in hospital, on the child's being discharged; or they might make an approach as a result of what a parent tells the family doctor.

Social workers are always

able to advise on eligibility for state benefits. Indeed, such advice is often called for because many families are not aware of their rights to benefits. If, as a result of unexpected misfortune, a family has difficulty in paying rent or meeting fuel bills, the Social Services will help if at all possible and perhaps even pay such bills in cases of extreme need. The case-worker will almost always like to visit the home and discuss problems with those concerned in order to have a full understanding of the situation.

Social workers will also advise upon child minders, day nurseries, play-groups, services for the handicapped, rent rebates, employment opportunities and a host of other matters. Those in need of advice on legal matters or marriage guidance will be given practical help: if the case-worker cannot help a client themselves, they will put him or her in touch with an organization that can, and introduce the two parties to each other.

The address of the nearest local-authority office of the Social Services department can be found in the telephone directory.

**Health visitors**

Health visitors are usually attached to a family doctor's practice, health centre or maternity and child-health clinic. One of their main functions is to visit expectant and nursing mothers and advise them on the care of young children.

**One-parent families**

National Council for
One-parent Families
255 Kentish Town Road
London NW5 2LX
01-267 1361

Scottish Council for Single
Parents
44 Albany Street
Edinburgh EH1 3QR
031-556 3899
Advice, information and counselling for lone parents.

Gingerbread
35 Wellington Street
London WC2
01-240 0953
This organization provides information and support for lone parents. There are over 250 self-help groups throughout Britain.

Life
35 Kenilworth Road
Leamington Spa
Warwickshire
0926 21587
This organization provides confidential counselling and practical help, including accommodation, for unsupported pregnant women. There are 150 branches.

**Adoption and fostering**

The Association of British
Adoption and Fostering
Agencies
4 Southampton Row
London WC1B 4AA
01-242 8951
The association gives general advice on adoption.

Parent-to-Parent Information
26 Belsize Grove
London NW3
01-722 5328
This is an organization of adoptive and prospective adoptive parents and of interested social workers. It has about 50 clubs throughout Britain.

National Foster Care Association
80 Belmont Park
Lewisham
London SE13 5BN
This is a self-help organization of over 100 local groups that provides support and advice for foster parents.

**Organizations for special disabilities**

(arranged in alphabetical order of disability or condition)

The National Society for
Autistic Children
1a Golders Green Road
London NW1 8EA
01-458 4375
The society has 30 local branches.

Royal National Institute for
the Blind
224 Great Portland Street
London W1N 6AA
01-388 1266

The Coeliac Society
P.O. Box 181
London NW2 2QY

The Cystic Fibrosis Research
Trust
5 Blyth Road
Bromley
Kent
01-464 7211
The trust has 200 local branches.

National Deaf Children's
Society
31 Gloucester Place
London W1H 4EA
01-486 3251
The society has 60 local associations.

Down's Children's Association
Quinborne Community Centre
Ridgeacre Road
Birmingham B32 2TW
021-427 1374
This association is for the parents of mongol children.

National Society for Mentally
Handicapped Children
Pembridge Hall
17 Pembridge Square
London, WC2 4EP

01-229 8941
The society has 400 local groups.

The British Epilepsy Association
3-6 Alfred Place
London WC1E 7ED
01-580 2704
The association has 80 local branches.

Invalid Children's Aid Association
126 Buckingham Palace Road
London SW1W 9SB
01-730 9891

Muscular Dystrophy Group
Nattrass House
35 Macaulay Road
London SW4 0QP
01-720 8055
The group has 275 local branches.

The National Society for Phenylketonuria and Allied Disorders
46 Towngate Grove
Mirfield
West Yorkshire
092-856 5081

The Spastics Society
12 Park Crescent
London W1N 4EQ
01-636 5020
The society has over 180 local groups.

Association for All Speech-impaired Children
Room 14
Toynbee Hall
28 Commercial Street
London E1 6LS
01-247 1497

Association for Spina Bifida and Hydrocephalus
Tavistock House North
Tavistock Square
London WC1H 9HJ
01-388 1382
There are over 70 local associations.

**General**

Pre-school Play-groups Association
Alford House
Aveline Street
London SE11 5DH
01-582 8871
The association has over 8,000 affiliated play-groups.

NSPCC (National Society for the Prevention of Cruelty to Children)
1 Riding House Street
London W1P 8AA
01-580 8812
(Consult telephone directory for address of nearest office.)
The society offers help and advice to parents with problems, investigates reports of neglect and ill-treatment of children and takes action when necessary.

Child Poverty Action Group
1 Macklin Street
Drury Lane
London WC2B 5NH
01-242 3225
The group has 70 branches throughout the country with staff qualified to advise on welfare rights, etc. For enquiries about rights to national insurance benefit, contact the Citizens' Rights office at the above address or telephone 01-405 5942/4517.

**Bereavement**

Cruse (National Organization for Widows and Children)
126 Sheen Road
Richmond
Surrey TW9 1UR
01-940 4818

Foundation for the Study of Infant Deaths
23 St Peter's Square
London W6 9NW
01-235 1721 (day)
01-748 7768 (evening)
The foundation gives information, support and reassurance to bereaved parents.

# Children's libraries

In most large towns and cities in the UK there is an extensive library service which caters for all ages, including the pre-school child. These services for children are usually part of the main library, although in some areas they may be housed in a separate building. Any local library can provide information on children's library services. Children's librarians can be extremely helpful. They are fully trained librarians who are additionally qualified to advise on books for children of all ages; they are also very approachable and used to dealing with children.

Most children's libraries have schemes whereby they allocate books in bulk to pre-school play-groups, day nurseries (whether private or run by the local authority), and even to recognized child minders. It is worth enquiring about this facility, which is not always well publicized.

Many children's libraries have story-telling sessions for pre-school children. These are usually well advertised in the library.

Some libraries even arrange small film-and slide-shows on appropriate topics for young children.

The local library is also a valuable source of information relating to local facilities and activities, especially those for pre-school children. There will usually be a booklet containing lists of play-groups, of both private and local-authority day nurseries, of facilities for handicapped children and even of local branches of special societies such as the British Diabetic Association, the Spastic Society, and so on, compiled by such interested parties as mothers of pre-school children in conjunction with the Social Services and community child-health services. Most booklets include a list of every infant welfare clinic in the vicinity, too, and provide other useful information such as how to register with a doctor and where to obtain a list of all family doctors in the area.

Some libraries have a mobile section for children. The mobile library can visit the homes of sick or handicapped children, making the use of library facilities far easier for children or parents in this situation.

# Book list

The list of books given below is not comprehensive but will cover most aspects of child care, mainly in the pre-school area but sometimes beyond this period. The list is provided for those who, having read this book, might care to extend their knowledge of certain areas of child care. Some of the books are intended primarily for parents or for teachers; others are somewhat more technical but interesting nonetheless.

It must be emphasized that the complete and perfect book of child care will never exist. Nonetheless, some excellent books have been written. Some, such as Dr Spock's and Hugh Jolly's, inevitably reflect the personality of the author; theirs are comprehensive works of reference aimed primarily at parents, and are not intended to be read from cover to cover in a short space of time. Other books, such as John Bowlby's *Child Care and the Growth of Love*, are more philosophical and are worth reading from beginning to end in order to understand the author's point of view.

Many of the books listed below can be found in public libraries; if not actually in stock, they can usually be obtained on request.

**Book of Child Care,** Hugh Jolly, Sphere Books, 1977, £1·95.
This is the best and most comprehensive book on child care in the English language.

**Baby and Child Care,** Benjamin Spock, New English Library, 1969, 75p.
This is the American equivalent of Hugh Jolly's book and was the first in its field.

**Babyhood,** Penelope Leach, Penguin, 1976, £1·50.

**Babies and Young Children** R.S. and C.M. Illingworth, Churchill-Livingstone, 1972, £3·95.

**The Normal Child,** R.S. Illingworth, Churchill-Livingstone, 1978, £6.
An excellent book for both parents and doctors.

**Common Ailments in Babies,** R.S. Illingworth, British Medical Association (a Family Doctor booklet), 25p.
A short but useful account of minor ailments in babies.

**Development of the Infant and Young Child, Normal and Abnormal,** R.S. Illingworth, Churchill-Livingstone, 1972, £5·50.
A fairly detailed account of child development, rather more medical in its approach.

**The Child at School,** R.S. Illingworth, Blackwell Scientific Publications, 1974, £5.
This book is primarily aimed at teachers but is worthwhile reading for parents, too.

**Lessons from Childhood: some aspects of the early life of unusual men and women,** C.M. Illingworth, Churchill-Livingstone, 1966, £3.

**Infant feeding,** Mavis Gunther, Penguin, 1973, 30p.
A useful and informative account of infant feeding.

**Infant Feeding and Feeding Difficulties,** Ronald MacKeith and Christopher Wood, Churchill-Livingstone, 1977, £6·50.
This book is intended for doctors and nurses to aid them in the diagnosis and management of feeding disorders, but is also interesting reading for parents.

**The First Nine Months of Life,** Geraldine Lux-Flanagan, Heinemann, 1975, £2·60.

**Developmental Progress of Infants and Young Children,** Mary Sheridan, Her Majesty's Stationery Office, 1968, 45p.
This is a detailed account of the developmental attainments of children up to the age of five.

**Child Care and the Growth of Love,** John Bowlby, Penguin, 1970, 60p.

**Attachment and Loss,**
volumes 1 (1969) and 2 (1973), John Bowlby, Hogarth Press, £4 each.
Both the above titles by John Bowlby relate to separations and their effect on the child.

**Twins,** Carola Zenter, David and Charles, 1975, £3·95.
This is a useful book for parents about the practical and philosophical problems of raising twins.

**Diabetic Children,**
J.W. Farquhar, Churchill-Livingstone, 1975, 75p.

**How Children Grow,**
(volume 1), Mark Lovell, Routledge and Kegan Paul, 1975, £1·75.
This book is concerned in particular with psychological development and the way in which the personality develops.

**Instructional games**
A whole range of educational materials for the pre-school child is published by Macdonald 3 4 5. It includes reading, counting, sorting and matching games, all in bold, colourful designs and priced at around £1. For details, contact Macdonald Educational at the address on p. 2.

**Magazines**
Child care is frequently discussed in many of the popular women's magazines such as *Woman, Woman's Own, Woman's Realm,* and so on. Other magazines, including *Parents, Mother, Mother and Baby, Maternity and Mothercraft, Under Five* and *Contact*, the magazine of the Pre-School Play-groups Association, are specifically concerned with the subject of child care and development.

# Glossary

**Acidosis:** an accumulation of acid in the blood, usually following severe diarrhoea.
**Adenoid:** a collection of germ-destroying (lymphoid) tissue at the back of the nose and next to the Eustachian tube, *q.v.*
**Allergy:** sensitivity to a foreign substance, usually producing a rash, swelling of eyelids or lips, or wheezing.
**Anoxia:** a deficiency of oxygen in the blood.
**Antibiotic:** a drug which either kills bacterial germs or prevents them multiplying.
**Antibody:** a naturally produced substance which attacks and destroys foreign proteins such as bacterial germs in the body.
**Anus:** the back passage; the end of the alimentary canal where the bowel opens.
**Appendicitis:** an acute illness in which the appendix becomes swollen and inflamed.
**Appendix:** a small finger-like extension from the beginning of the large bowel.
**Asthma:** a disorder of breathing, characterized by wheezing and shortness of breath. Usually allergic in origin.
**Bacterium:** a type of germ which is enclosed by a membrane and can survive inside or outside the cells of the body. Responds to antibiotics.
**Bottom shuffling:** a curious form of progression adopted by some children in place of crawling. These children walk later than usual.
**Breath-holding attack:** a deliberate attempt (normally by a child) to hold one's breath to the point of unconsciousness. Though alarming, such attacks are harmless.
**Breech delivery:** a birth in which the baby is born bottom-first instead of head-first.
**Bronchi:** the bronchial tubes which convey air to the lungs.
**Bronchiolitis:** a severe breathing disorder of short duration, caused by a virus which produces inflammation of the smallest bronchial tubes (the bronchioles).
**Bronchitis:** an inflammation of the bronchial tubes, usually caused by a virus.
**Caput:** localized wrinkling and swelling of a new-born infant's scalp, produced by compression of the head during delivery.
**Care order:** a legal injunction transferring the care of and responsibility for a child's welfare from the parents to a third party (such as the Social Services). The injunction is usually made by a magistrate in a juvenile court.
**Caries:** tooth decay.
**Cell:** the basic unit of all living tissue.
**Cerebral palsy:** a condition resulting from brain damage that usually occurs during or soon after birth. It leads to spasticity (rigidity) of muscles and other problems.
**Child:** in law, a person who is less than fourteen years of age.
**Child benefit:** a weekly allowance paid by the government to all legal parents. It replaces the family allowance.
**Child minder:** a person who looks after a child by day for a working mother. To operate legally, child minders must be registered with the local authority.
**Croup:** an inflammation of the larynx (voice box) or windpipe which produces a crowing noise

when breathing. The condition is caused by a virus, *q.v.*

**Cystic fibrosis:** a disease, inherited from both parents, which causes difficulty in absorbing food properly and therefore prevents growth. It also causes severe chest infections.

**Day nursery:** a centre in which pre-school children are looked after during working hours. Day nurseries can be run either privately or by a local authority.

**Dehydration:** a deficiency of water in the body, usually caused by severe vomiting or diarrhoea.

**Demand feeding:** the practice of allowing a baby to feed when he is hungry rather than by the clock.

**Diabetes:** a disease in which the sugar in the blood is not used up properly. Children with this condition need insulin by injection.

**Diarrhoea:** frequent passage of watery bowel motions.

**Down's syndrome:** the medical term for mongolism, *q.v.*

**DPT:** diphtheria-pertussis-tetanus vaccine; the so-called three-in-one or 'triple' immunization.

**Eczema:** a skin condition found in allergic patients, especially asthmatic children.

**Electric toothbrush:** an automatic device, usually battery-powered, to which a small toothbrush is attached.

**Enuresis:** the medical term for bed-wetting in those over five years of age.

**Epiglottis:** a small fold of cartilage which protects the entrance to the windpipe.

**Epiglottitis:** inflammation of the epiglottis producing croup and breathing difficulties.

**Eustachian tube:** a small passage connecting the back of the throat to the cavity behind the ear drum.

**Family allowance:** see *child benefit.*

**Family income supplement:** an addition to the basic income provided by the state in the case of working parents who earn very little (see p. 84).

**Fat necrosis:** small areas of hard, congealed fat, the size of a ball bearing, which usually occur on the face; they are caused by forceps pressure at birth, soon disappear and are of no medical significance.

**Febrile convulsion:** a fit which is caused by a fever.

**Fever:** a body temperature greater than 37·6°C (98·4°F).

**Fissure in ano:** a split in the lining of the anus. Such a split could lead to constipation.

**Fluoride:** an essential dietary element for the formation of strong tooth enamel.

**Fontanelle:** the diamond-shaped 'soft spot' on the top of a new-born infant's head.

**Gastro-enteritis:** diarrhoea with or without vomiting, caused by bowel infection.

**Glucose:** one of several sugars found in the body, and the most important in man: it is found in all body fluids except urine.

**Glue ear:** a collection of fluid behind the ear drum. It is caused by infection and may result in hearing loss.

**Grommet:** a small plastic tube placed in the ear drum to allow glue ears to drain.

**Guardian ad litem:** an independent individual appointed by the courts to represent the specific interests of a particular child.

**Head banging:** habit of banging the head against hard surfaces, such as a wall or cot. It is most commonly seen among young children who are emotionally deprived.

**Health visitor:** an employee of the area health authority who is qualified to advise on health matters for people of all ages and who visits homes for this purpose (see pp. 20-22).

**Heart murmur:** an unusual noise originating from the heart which can only be heard with a stethoscope. It does not necessarily imply heart disease.

**House-dust mite:** a microscopic mite which lives on skin scales and provokes asthma in some susceptible subjects.

**Hyaline membraine disease:** a breathing disorder which occurs in some pre-term infants and can be severe.

**Hydrocele:** an abnormal collection of fluid between the testicle and its coverings. The condition is harmless.

**Hyperactivity:** continuous physical activity which never ceases regardless of surroundings. It may be the result of brain damage.

**Immunization:** the production of immunity to certain diseases by inoculating the patient with either a dead, inactivated sample of the germ that causes the disease, or a harmless germ of the same family.

**Infant:** a child under one year of age.

**Infant welfare clinic:** a medical centre run by the area health authority to supervise the health of infants. The clinics provide only advice, not treatment.

**Infectious disease:** those illnesses that can be communicated from person to person; the term generally implies those which can occur in epidemic form, such as measles.

**Intubation:** the passage of a tube down the windpipe to establish breathing at birth. Such treatment is only necessary on occasions.

**Jargon speech:** a peculiar and individual way of speaking, unintelligible to strangers, which is common in young children.

**Jaundice:** a yellow discoloration of the skin caused

by a pigment that builds up when the liver is not working properly.

**Koplik's spots:** small, greyish spots, like grains of salt, which are seen in the mouth just before the measles rash appears.

**Lanugo:** fine hair on the body of pre-term infants that disappears in due course.

**Larynx:** the voice-box (the Adam's apple in adults).

**Laryngitis:** inflammation of the voice-box.

**Low birth-weight:** a weight of less than 2·5 kg (5 lb 8 oz) at birth.

**Lumbar puncture:** removal of fluid from the spinal canal by a needle inserted into the lower back. This procedure is used for diagnosing meningitis.

**Lymph glands:** small glands, found in the neck, armpits, groin and many other areas, which serve to remove germs from the body. The glands enlarge when performing this function.

**Malformation:** abnormally formed organ or part of the body.

**Maturity:** in medicine, the age of the fetus or new-born infant.

**Meningitis:** a serious disease caused by infection of the coverings of the brain.

**Mesenteric adenitis:** swelling of the lymph glands inside the abdomen. This condition may mimic appendicitis.

**Mid-parent height:** the average height of a child's two parents.

**Milestone:** in medicine, a developmental attainment for a given age.

**Milia:** small, blocked sweat glands seen on face of some new-born infants.

**Mongolism:** a generalized abnormality, present at birth. Mongoloid children have a distinctive face and are mentally retarded.

**Moro reflex:** 'startle' response seen in new-born babies, in which the arms fly out and are then crossed across the body. This response is normally always present in the new-born.

**Mumps:** an infectious disease affecting the parotid (salivary) glands of the face.

**NAI:** medical term for non-accidental injury to a child, popularly termed baby-battering.

**Neonate:** new-born; an infant of less than one month of age.

**New-born:** see *neonate*.

**Night terrors:** distressing, repetitive nightmares that cause acute fear.

**Obesity:** extreme corpulence; condition of being severely overweight.

**Otitis media:** an infection of the middle ear, which is behind the ear drum.

**Paediatrician:** a specialist doctor with a hospital appointment who treats children and their diseases.

**Phenylketonuria (PKU):** a disease causing mental retardation. The mental retardation can be prevented if the condition is diagnosed early.

**Placenta:** the after-birth and organ of nutrition for the unborn baby.

**Place of safety order:** legal injunction that removes parental rights for up to twenty-eight days and transfers them to the Social Services.

**Pneumonia:** an infection of the lungs, usually caused by a bacteria germ. The infection is less serious now than formerly.

**Pre-term:** of babies, born before thirty-seven weeks of pregnancy have been completed.

**Prophylactic:** a measure of any kind which is taken to prevent disease.

**Quarantine:** that period of time when a child with an infectious disease can transmit it to others.

**Retrolental fibroplasia:** a condition, found in premature babies, that is caused by too much oxygen in the blood.

**Rickets:** a bone disease caused by lack of Vitamin D.

**Rooming in:** hospital accommodation for a baby beside the mother as opposed to in a nursery.

**Rubella:** the medical term for german measles.

**Scald:** a burn caused by a hot liquid or gas.

**School-phobia:** pathological dislike of and non-attendance at school. This can be a serious psychiatric problem.

**Seborrhoeic dermatitis:** a skin rash affecting scalp and face and sometimes other areas.

**Small-for-dates:** unusually small for the length of the pregnancy.

**Soiling:** leaking of small amounts of stool. This habit is psychological, not medical, in origin.

**Sticky eye:** an inflammation with discharge from the eyelids. The condition is fairly common amongst the new-born.

**Stork mark:** a reddish discoloration of the eyelids, the forehead, between the eyes and nape of neck, at birth. The discoloration fades after a few months.

**Threadworm:** a small worm which infests the lower bowel causing anal itching. Threadworms are common among young children.

**Trachea:** the medical term for the windpipe.

**Umbilicus:** the area of the abdomen, through which the umbilical cord is attached.

**Ventilator:** a breathing machine used for the treatment of severe respiratory disorders.

**Vernix:** a cheesy material present on the skin of new-born infants.

**Virus:** a germ which does not respond to antibiotics and can survive only inside a living cell.

**Weaning:** the transition from milk to solid food.

# Index

Numbers in italics indicate captions

# Credits

**Artists**
Barry Kemp
Sally Launder
Ron Hayward
Robin Drury

**Photographs**
Burghardt & Degenhardt for Raleigh Industries Ltd, 42 (right)
John Garrett, 7, 50, 62
John Golden, 8, 9, 10, 11, 17, 40, 41, 69 (bottom)
Henry Grant, AIIP, 6
Richard and Sally Greenhill, 32, 33, 34, 35, 39, 43, 61, 64, 65, 75, 78, 80
Raymond Irons Photography, 51
Barry Kemp, 13, 18, 31, 38, 42 (left), 63, 68, 69 (top)
John Kingaby Associates, 67
Margaret Murray, 71
Peter Myers, 21
PAF International, 66
Pictorial Press, 60, 79
Zefa, 5

**Cover**
Photograph: Peter Myers